ZANY CHARACTERS OF THE AD WORLD

COLLECTOR'S IDENTIFICATION & VALUE GUIDE

MARY JANE LAMPHIER

COLLECTOR BOOKS

A Division of Schroeder Publishing Co., Inc.

The current values in this book should be used only as a guide. They are not intended to set prices, which vary from one section of the country to another. Auction prices as well as dealer prices vary greatly and are affected by condition as well as demand. Neither the Author nor the Publisher assumes responsibility for any losses that might be incurred as a result of consulting this guide.

On the cover:
Arby's Characters, "Hargreaves Lic. By NEA," $3.00 each.
Bicentennial Campbell Kids, Campbell Soup Co.®, $35.00 each.
McDonald's Ronald, McDonald's Corporation, $25.00.

Searching For A Publisher?

We are always looking for knowledgeable people considered to be experts within their fields. If you feel that there is a real need for a book on your collectible subject and have a large comprehensive collection, contact Collector Books.

Book design by Gina Lage
Cover design by Beth Summers

Additional copies of this book may be ordered from:

COLLECTOR BOOKS
P.O. Box 3009
Paducah, Kentucky 42002–3009
or
Mary Jane Lamphier
577 Main St.
Arlington, IA 50606

@$16.95. Add $2.00 for postage and handling.

Copyright: Mary Jane Lamphier, 1995

CONTENTS

ACKNOWLEDGMENTS

Throughout this book, corporate trademarks have been used in compliance with the rights of trademarks as stated by the International Trademark Association. To ensure registered marks will be recognized as corporate trademarks, the first use of each mark will be followed by the ® symbol. Each trademark name and character used in this book is owned and registered by the company listed and cannot be used in any other form.

Information Received Directly from the Following Companies

Brown & Williamson Tobacco
   Corporation
B & W Background Information
Realizing Tomorrow's Strategies Today

Campbell Soup Company
"The Founding Years"
"The Campbell Kid History"
Newsletters on Vlasic Foods

Chase Packaging Corp.
(Chase Bag Company)
Reidsville, NC

Coca-Cola Company Archives
Atlanta, Georgia

Dakin Inc.
Linda Dalton, Marketing

Eveready Battery Company
Eveready, The Battery Story

Farmers & Merchants Savings Bank
"Moola Moola and the Money
   Minders"

Foreign Candy Company
"The Company History"

Frito-Lay
"Marketing Case History" on
   GrandMa's Brand Cookies®

General Mills
Jean Toll, Corporate Archivist

Grand Metropolitan
Sally Selby, Consumer Relations

Iowa Credit Union League Services
   Corporation
"What is the Kirby Kangaroo Club?"

Kellogg's
"Chronology of Dolls Offered as
   Premiums"

Lever Brothers Company
Sheryl Zapic, Public Relations
   Coordinator

Lincoln Savings Bank
Lincoln Savings Bank 75th Anniversary

Little Crow Foods
Elizabeth A. Cote, Consumer
   Representative

Maytag Corporation
Maytag Corporation 1992 Annual Report
The Spark of Enterprise, a History of Dixie
   Foundry — Magic Chef Inc.

Mattel Inc.
Lisa McKendall, Marketing
   Communications

McDonald's
"The House That Love Builds, Ronald
   McDonald House"

McKee Company
Janet Grabowski

Michelin Tire Co.
"The Bibendum Story"
BIB America

Planters Lifesavers Company
Lynora Essic, Consumer Representative

Pillsbury
Pillsbury, To Be the Best

Renk Seed Company
Steven E. Renk, President

S.C. Johnson & Sons Inc.
Julie Richardson, Assistant
   Brand Manager

Sherwin Williams
Return of the Dutch Boy

StarKist Seafood
Ken Schockman, Consumer Relations
   Representative

Uhlmann Company
Jay Rasmussen

United States Postal Service
Joe Rogers, Retailing Marketing
   Specialist

Wolverine World Wide Inc.
A Tradition of Success

Woodland Enterprises
The Woodland Catalog

People and Companies that Donated Characters

A & W Root Beer, Steve Waskow
Campbell Soup Company
Chase Bag Company
Ginger Darling
Dakin Inc.
Gary Doden
Foreign Candy Company
Barbara Gerdes
Alice Hunt

Iowa Credit Union League
Mary Kangas
Kellogg Co.
Kum & Go
Lamphier Brothers
Lever Brothers
Little Crow Foods
Becky Loop
Heather Lukin

Mattel Inc.
Michelin Company
Megan Moats
S.C. Johnson & Sons Inc.
Rowena Smith
Vicky Seedorf
Jean Turner
Jo Turner

My first advertising doll was a gift from a neighbor. Jo Turner doesn't realize what she started! Before this, I was never involved in advertising. In fact, I viewed advertising as expensive propaganda. Advertising t-shirts were ridiculous! Decorating with advertising, tacky-tacky!

Advertising definitely was not a part of my life until Mohawk Tommy took up residence. I developed a new curiosity, a passion for particulars. Who designed the doll? Who made the doll? How was it available to consumers? Solving the mystery and researching was a challenge. After the case was closed I began making "research" trips, hunting for more ad characters. The mute button was no longer pushed during commercials. Do you know there is nothing worth watching on TV now *except* the commercials?

The songs, the art, the zany characters are wonderful...entertaining and witty. The people who create the commercials should be commended (I am sure they are remunerated) for the brilliant display, the imagination, and creativity.

Commercials give me insight on what three dimensional characters to look for: Bart Simpson™ advertising Butterfinger® Candy Bars, the California Raisins®, the Noid® from Dominos Pizza®, and others.

As the collection of advertising characters accumulated, I began writing a weekly column, "Zany Characters of the Ad World," for *Collectors Journal*, in 1991.

My second home became the Hendersen-Wilder Library at Upper Iowa University, in Fayette, Iowa. Mary White, the librarian, was most helpful. I read many old periodicals that revealed a treasure of pioneer advertising and product history.

One of the first free mail-in premiums found was in a 1905 *Ladies' Home Journal* (see advertisement on right). A rag doll made by Art Fabric Mills was the prize. The doll was done in oil colors on fine, strong cloth. The ad stated, "the colors will not crock." The "most forceful ad ever written" is as follows:

> *We will send you the Doll postpaid* — Free of expense. *We want to know how many JOURNAL readers answer advertisements. We have spent hundreds of thousands of dollars in advertising our Cloth Toys, and we want to know just how many readers would respond to the most forceful ad ever written...*

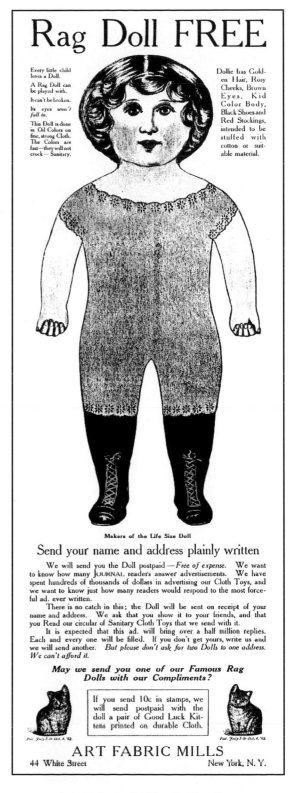

Art Fabric Mills Doll offer.
Ladies' Home Journal, **October 1905.**

Aunt Jemima Rag Doll Family offer.
Ladies' Home Journal, December 1916.

Aunt Jemima Family, 1925. Photo courtesy of Allen Meeker.

The Aunt Jemima Mills Company began offering "Special Rag Dolls" as early as 1916, (see ad at left from *The Ladies' Home Journal*, December 1916). The family of four Black dolls was free with a 10¢ stamp. These dolls were trademarks of the Aunt Jemima Mills Company in St. Joseph, Missouri. Allen Meeker submitted the photograph (below left) of three of the Aunt Jemima Rag Doll Family advertised in 1925.

Subscription dolls were popular in the 1930's. *Ladies' Home Journal* offered free dolls to anyone that sold four one-year subscriptions. The dolls were the popular dolls of the era. Some offered were Shirley Temple, Sonja Henie, and Deanna Durbin. (See the ads on page 7.)

A cloth "Little Lulu," a famous *Saturday Evening Post* cartoon character at the time, was offered to people selling two one-year subscriptions. The doll is 17" tall. (See the ad on page 8.)

Premiums are designed to promote sales. They introduce new products and draw attention to old products. Some companies continue to offer premiums of the trademark image, such as the Campbell Kids® (Chapter Four). Other companies pick up famous figures and make a deal with the copyright holder, such as the Walt Disney characters in Chapter Two.

Container premiums are the reusable packaging like the Donald Duck bank in Chapter One and the bottles worth saving in Chapter Three.

Packaged premiums include the extra gifts with the product. Cereal companies enjoy adding little treasures in the box of cereal. Occasionally the gift is large, such as the Batman bank, and it is shrink-wrapped to the cereal box.

WIN THIS ROYAL GIFT!
"Shirley Temple" Doll with Outfit!

Any little girl will adore having a "Shirley Temple" doll, 13 inches tall and daintily dressed.

But imagine her joy at also receiving our special Outfit, including Party Dress, "Heidi" dress copied from the recent motion picture, Coat and Hat with Pocketbook, Pajamas and extra set of Underwear.

All these articles are copies of Shirley's own clothes and will fit the 13-inch doll exactly.

Win both Doll and Outfit by sending seven 1-year *Ladies' Home Journal* subscriptions, sold at $1 each. Or you may

win both for four 1-year subscriptions for *The Saturday Evening Post*, sold at $2 each.

Either Doll or Outfit will be sent separately for four 1-year *Journal* or two 1-year *Post* subscriptions. (Subscriptions which qualify for either prize, must be sold to persons living outside your own home.)

Pin subscribers' names and addresses, with your own, to this ad and *state whether you want both Doll and Outfit, or Doll only.* Then inclose check or money order for full amount and send to

CURTIS PUBLISHING COMPANY, 848 Independence Square, Phila., Pa.

NOTE: *Doll will be sent to Canada, but we cannot send Outfit.*

Shirley Temple dolls subscription offer. *Ladies' Home Journal,* **January 1938.**

Continuity-point premiums are those gifts requiring a number of points, such as the Wacky WareHouse® catalog collection. The points are saved from all Kool-Aid® products.

Qualifiers may range from postage and UPCs to the retail cost of the premium. To help promote purchasing of the product rather than trading of qualifiers, the cash register receipt is often required.

Fast food restaurants are notorious for offering free premiums with meals to encourage traffic. The toys may be free or they may be sold at a discount. Complete books are written on the subject of McDonald's — I have included some McDonald's trademark characters but very few, for this reason. There is also a sample of Wendy's, Burger King, Hardee's, and Arby's premiums in this book.

Another type of advertising is the retailed trademark character. Barney® and the Cabbage Patch Kid® banks are in this category.

Store displays are more expensive than some of the other ad characters. Old Crow®, with his top hat and red vest, is a favorite collectible. Three different figures are included in this book (see page 102).

Collectors may choose to collect only premiums, or displays, banks, dolls, figurines, or telephones. However most collectors of ad characters, that I know, are not dis-

Sonja Henic and Deanna Durbin dolls subscription offer. *Ladies' Home Journal,* **December 1939.**

This "Sonja Henie" Skating Doll is the year's sensation. Dressed in white taffeta with marabou trim, she stands 15 inches tall on her tiny skates.

Your Choice!

IF SANTA doesn't slip one of these beauties into your little girl's stocking, it just won't be Christmas!

Yours . . . either beautiful doll . . . if you send only four 1-year *Ladies' Home Journal* subscriptions sold at the full price, $1 each, to persons living outside your own home. Or send two 1-year *Saturday Evening Posts,* sold at the full price, $2 each. (This Offer good in U. S. and Canada.)

Pin subscribers' names and addresses to coupon below and mail with check or money order for full amount.

Fourteen inches tall, her wavy brown hair, blue eyes, adorable dimples make this "Deanna Durbin" doll the image of her namesake. Dress is a copy of one worn in a hit picture.

CURTIS PUBLISHING COMPANY
234 Independence Square, Phila., Penna.

Here are .... subscriptions with remittance.

Send my .... doll, all charges prepaid, to

Name ....

Street ....

City .... State ....

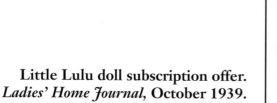

Little Lulu doll subscription offer.
Ladies' Home Journal, **October 1939.**

This "Lulu" doll . . . 17 inches tall with soft body, flexible legs, and the tantalizing expression that "Lulu" wears in the Post's famous cartoons!

FOR YOU—

TO WIN "Lulu" send two 1-year *Ladies' Home Journal* subscriptions which you have sold at the full price, $1 each, to persons living outside your own home. Or send two 1-year *Posts*, sold at $2 each. (Offer good in U. S. and Canada.) Pin subscribers' names and addresses with your own to this ad. Then mail with check or money order to CURTIS PUBLISHING COMPANY, 955 Independence Square, Philadelphia, Pennsylvania.

criminating. It is more common that once they get caught up with collecting advertising characters anything goes! If a collector is really hooked, he or she may get into other advertising too, such as the Mr. Peanut® tinware to display with the dolls, banks, and figural salt and pepper shakers.

Many companies have provided information for this book. Some have also included the advertising character with the information, of which I am most grateful. Friends and family have donated characters also and I have listed the donators separately. If any were forgotten it was not intentional. These people have made the task of compiling this guide much easier.

Other people, too numerous to list by name, have donated coupons, UPCs, ads for dolls, and other qualifiers so that I might continue collecting zany characters for this book.

Collectors in New York, Florida, Illinois, Minnesota, Ohio, Tennessee, Kansas, and Iowa have helped locate items on my "wish list." Some have traded items, others have made their treasures available for photographs.

A special thank you to Lisa Stroup and the staff at Collector Books that made this book possible.

While collecting and writing I have become more knowledgeable on consumerism and advertising and much of what I have learned I am passing on to other collectors. The more information one has on a collectible, the more interesting it is to the collector.

The prices listed are basically this writer's opinion. It will provoke questions and debates as prices are governed by location, condition, availability, and demand. The majority of prices are my cost of the item plus appreciation of a collectible that happens to be a "hot" item at this time. Other prices are an average taken from guides on the market and dealer's shops.

One fact learned after years of collecting advertising characters is that no book can possibly include all and every collectible. Collecting and writing may be life long projects!

CHAPTER ONE

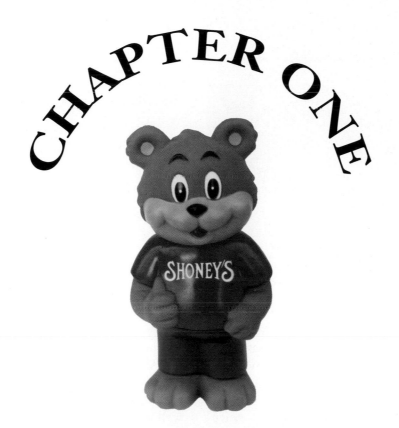

Advertising & Trademark Banks

ADMIRAL

Admiral — 1970's
The Admiral Corporation, 7", vinyl, $20.00.

It was 1934, the year Emilie, Yvonne, Celie, Marie, and Annette Dionne were born. The favorite boardgame Monopoly was invented by Charles Darrow, and commercial radio stations were in full swing in America. Every household had to have at least one radio.

The time was right for two young Chicago entrepreneurs, Ross David Siragusa and his cousin Vincent Barreca, to capitalize on the public demand for radios. They started their business in a garage and proceeded to make five-tube radios. They sold the radios for $9.95 each. In two years Siragusa and Barreca realized sales of two million dollars.

They expanded with more styles of radios and they added phonographs. By 1941, there was no evidence of hard times in "brown goods" sales. The Admiral Corporation had reached the $9.3 million sales mark!

In 1944 the Admiral Corporation started selling "white goods," Admiral refrigerators and stoves. Four years later a television line was added. The company reached its peak in 1950 with $18 million in sales. The next ten years was a different story. More competition and less demand contributed to a decline in profits until the company was operating in the red. In the 70's Siragusa was looking for a buyer for the Admiral Corporation.

Al Rockwell of Rockwell International Corporation purchased the Admiral Corporation in 1974 but Admiral continued to operate at a loss. Five years later Rockwell was ready to sell the appliance company.

Skeet Rymer from Magic Chef Inc. bought both Admiral and Norge in 1979 and the company prospered over the next seven years.

When Rymer approached the 50th year with Magic Chef, he was about ready to retire. He felt it would be wise to make a change in Magic Chef Inc. and in 1986 Magic Chef merged with Maytag, an Iowa based company.

Admiral banks were a part of promotional planning in the Admiral Company. They were given to customers with the purchase of an appliance. The bank is 7" tall. It is made of vinyl; clothes and features are molded and painted. Admiral portrays an early American with what appears to be a white wig under a black admiral's hat. The blue coat is trimmed with gold, and the white vest has gold buttons. White trousers and black shoes complete the costume.

Barney & Baby Bop — 1992
The Lyons Group®, 7½", vinyl, $10.00 each.

Barney, "A friend to you and me®," started taking the crayon crowd by storm in 1988 when he debuted in home videos.

Picture this scenario: a small stuffed dinosaur, the color of a ripe plum, transforms into a life-sized creature, at least six-feet tall. He proceeds to transport his Backyard Gang (children 7–12) to exciting places like the North Pole, the bottom of the ocean, and the moon! Everyone is having fun as Barney chuckles his way through one adventure after another.

Who deserves the credit for this delightful mixture of fantasy and reality? Sheryl Leach and Kathy Parker. Barney was their idea. Look what they do in "Barney Goes to School." Everyone sings with a happy heart: "If all the raindrops were lemon drops and gumdrops, oh what a rain that would be." They have puppet shows and finger painting. The kids have a wonderful attitude! They love school and want to go on Saturdays too.

In 1990 more children were exposed to Barney's magic through the Disney Channel. The pre-schoolers tuned into the "Lunch Box" series for daily reinforcement on how to get along in society with proper manners, learning the alphabet, and all kinds of good stuff.

Barney became famous after his PBS episodes in "Barney and Friends," and with fame comes diversification. Since Barney's debut, several Barney books are out: *Barney's Favorite Mother Goose Rhymes*, *Just Imagine*, *Barney's Hats*, and *Baby Bop's Toys*. Then, of course, the merchandisers began to capitalize on the lovable dinosaur.

Barney, the "Stuuuupendous" (Barney's favorite word) Tyrannosaurus Rex was showing up on everything from jogging outfits to toys. It was reported in *Time* magazine (Dec. 21, 1992) that President Bill Clinton bought a 4 foot Barney doll, Barney bed sheets, and underwear.

Collectors of advertising characters were snatching up Barney and Baby Bop molded vinyl banks. Barney is basically purple and his molded and painted clothing feature a white shirt and blue bag. Baby Bop is green with a purple hair ribbon and shoes. They are 7½" tall and well marked. Incised on the base of the bodies: "®1992 THE LYONS GROUP, MADE IN CHINA MANUF BY H.E.I." (H.E.I is Happiness Express Inc., a firm in New York, N.Y.)

BATMAN®

"Discover the delicious adventures awaiting you everyday with New Batman Cereal!"

In 1989 the Ralston Purina Company retailed a new presweetened cereal. It was a combination of wheat, corn, oat, and rice flours molded in the shape of a bat.

To enlighten consumers on the background of Batman, Bob Kane's comic book character, a short story was printed on the side of the box.

"In 1939 a new kind of super-hero was born. His name was The Batman. A dark, mysterious character of the night, stalking the streets, defying criminals with intelligence, athletic prowess, and state of the art gadgetry, terrifying enemies who dare cross his path.

The Batman had a secret identity, that of Bruce Wayne,™ wealthy playboy. At a very young age his parents were killed on the streets of Gotham City.™ Later, he used his inheritance to travel around the world, seeking out masters of justice and the martial arts, honing his body to perfection. A man whose obsession for justice gnawed at his soul. When he was ready, he returned to Gotham City,™ as The Batman, ready to terrorize the evil doers of the city and to avenge the death of his parents.

Fifty years later, Batman is still thrilling his fans with spectacular adventures, trailing criminals who wreak havoc on Gotham City.™"

In celebration of the 50th birthday of Batman and the beginning of the new Batman cereal, Ralston Purina included a Batman bank with the packaging.

The black plastic, molded bank has paper stickers to distinguish the facial features, the belt, and the symbol on the chest. "™ & ©DC Comics Inc. 1989" is printed on a paper label on the back. The bank is 7½" tall.

Batman — 1989
™ & ©DC Comics Inc., 7½", plastic, $5.00.

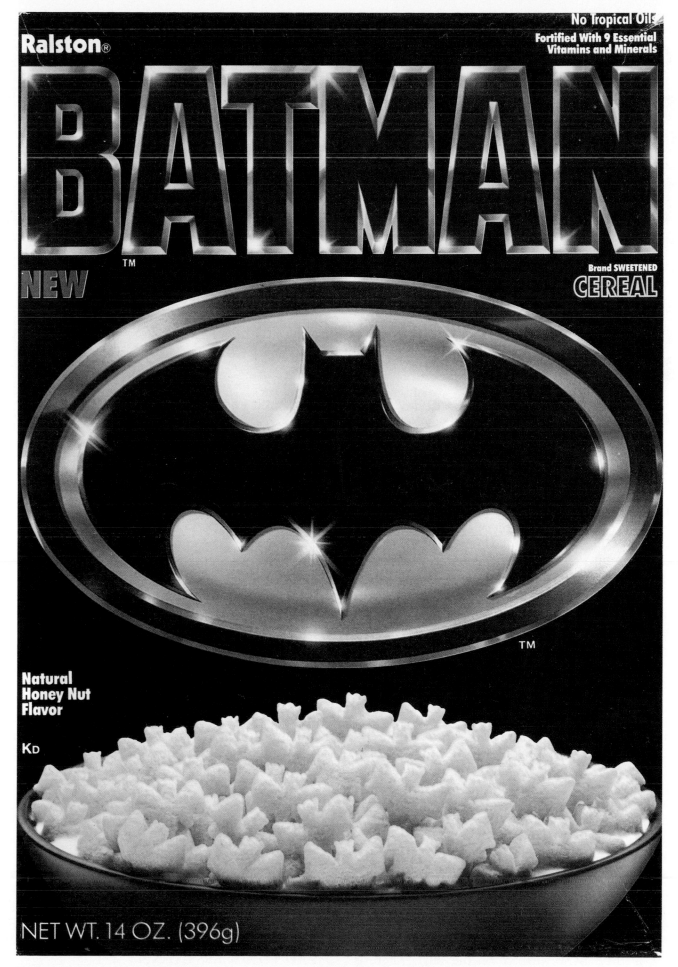

Batman™ Cereal, ©1989 DC Comics Inc., ©1989 Ralston Purina Co.

BIG BOY® & SHONEY BEAR®

Big Boy, Marriott Corporation, vinyl.
(A) 9", 1960's, $20.00. (B) 9", 1973, $20.00. C) 8", 1970's, $25.00.

Shoney Bear — 1993.
®Shoney's Inc., 8", vinyl, $12.00.

Big Boy was the brainchild of Bob Wain, a restaurant owner, as early as 1936. It did not happen over night but Bob's Big Boy Restaurants, in Glendale, California, developed into a national chain. Owners of the franchise were allowed to use first names as a prefix to Big Boy, consequently we find Shoney's Big Boy and others such as J.B.'s, and Elia's.

The mascot and trademark of the Big Boy Restaurants resembles a well fed boy with a Ronald Reagan hair style. The boy generally carries an oversized hamburger. His image decorates the inside of the restaurants and is used in advertising. It is not unusual to see a giant, three dimensional Big Boy at the front door of the restaurants.

In 1967 the Marriott Corporation bought the Big Boy restaurants, one of many new acquisitions. By 1977 Marriott operated 1,335 restaurants, 34 full service hotels, and 14 franchised inns. Marriott continued to move up and out. Buying competitor Howard Johnson Hotels in 1985 and developing "lifecare" communities in 1989 were two of many transactions.

During this time an assortment of trademark collectibles were offered at the restaurants for discount prices. One of the popular premiums was a molded vinyl bank. The head is flesh-tan vinyl with brown painted hair and painted features. Big Boy's trousers are the traditional white with red checks and suspenders to hold them up.

The first bank is molded in one piece. The only marking is "BIG BOY" printed on the shirt. There is no trademark identity or date. This bank was offered in the 60's or earlier, before the trademark image was trimmed down to match the healthy renovations of the new menus.

The second Big Boy banks were 9" tall and they were made much slimmer. The head and body were molded separate and legs are spread apart. By removing the head from the body, coins can be removed.

The "thin" Big Boy has incised on the bottom: "A PRODUCT OF BIG BOY RESTAURANTS OF AMERICA/Marriott Corp. 1973.

A third Big Boy, almost exactly like the second, has two noticeable differences. It is 8" tall and the name is written in script. The only marking is "Taiwan" incised on the bottom of one foot.

In the 1980's the corporation entertained the idea of eliminating the Big Boy symbol. The question was brought to the attention of the public and response was wonderful. The majority ruled: Big Boy remained on the scene.

Big Boy Restaurant managers were encouraged to use the Big Boy premium plan but there were some, of course, who had their own ideas. In the 90's we began to see Shoney Bears in some of the restaurants.

The molded plastic bear has a red painted shirt and blue trousers. It is 8" tall. Marks incised on the bottom of the feet: "SHONEY BEAR IS A/REGISTERED TRADEMARK ® OF/SHONEY'S INC./MADE IN CHINA/FOR AGES FOUR AND UP/REMOVE HEAD TO ACCESS COINS."

Del Monte Foods offered a number of trademark characters in the 1980's. People had to collect enormous amounts of UPCs to get free Country Yumkins®, Fluffy Lamb, Cocky Crow, Brawny Bear, Shoo Shoo Scare Crow and the Big Top Bonanza Clown Bank.

The bank is 7" tall and made of molded white plastic. Clothes and features are painted in bright primary colors. The clown has a yellow hat, red jacket, green trousers, and blue shoes. Marks on the base of the bank include: "BIG TOP BONANZA Del Monte 1985." "MADE IN TAIWAN" is molded in the bottom of the bank.

What is Del Monte doing almost a decade after the bank promotion? It's obvious they aren't clowning around! In a full page ad in the Sunday supplements, a beautiful two story home is bursting from a green can with a red "Del Monte" label. On the inside of the can's lid are the words, "YOU WIN A NEW HOME." Under the color picture, white lettering on black background states "Look under the lid of Del Monte Fruits, Vegetables or Tomatoes. You could win a new house! Prize awarded as $130,000."

The sweepstakes was open only to individuals whose primary residence is within the United States. Employees of Del Monte Foods, any of its affiliate companies, subsidiaries, agents, advertising agencies, suppliers, Gage Marketing Group, and immediate families of each were not eligible. The odds of winning the "Del Monte Under-the-lid Game" were 1:370,200,000. As contests go, it was short term. Game requests with complete rules and a free game piece ended March 31, 1994.

It would be interesting to know the facts and figures on this bonanza. Was the ultimate gimmick in advertising a successful venture? Del Monte will never tell!

Big Top Bonanza — 1985
Del Monte, 7", plastic, $10.00.

BLATZ BEER MEN®

"No jocks. No jokes. No cowboys. No horses. No mountains. No sunset. No tricks. No gimmicks. Nothing but great beer taste!" (An ad for Blatz Beer, in 1986.)

Advertising for Blatz was not always this simple. The Blatz Beer Men, anthropomorphic figures of three styles, were used to promote the product. One is short and fat with a beer barrel body. He has white hair and mustache. The second is taller and has a Blatz Beer can body. This character has auburn hair and one eye is shut in a mischievous wink. The third Blatz man has a tall slim Blatz Beer bottle body. It is a younger looking character with blond hair. All of them wear bow ties and usually carry a mug of foaming brew in one hand and a pennant in the other.

The three Blatz Beer Men trademarks have proclaimed the virtues of "Old Milwaukee's Finest Beer" in a variety of advertising methods including breweriana collectibles. Trays with the three Blatz Beer Men painted on them are very common.

The early pieces included cast iron figurals, banks, and wall displays, used as displays at points of sale. A 1968 metal store display features the three as "Blatz Baseball Players." In the 1950's and 1960's, the Blatz Beer Men are predominately plastic. A tin beer can or a glass bottle may be used in conjunction with plastic. All are easy to identify by the triangular "Blatz" label.

"MILWAUKEE'S FINEST BEER, BREWED AT MILWAUKEE, NEWARK, LOS ANGELES, PEORIA HEIGHTS" is printed on most of the collectibles except the cast iron characters.

The Blatz Beer Man Bank is heavy cast iron. The man measures 7½" in a sitting position. The metal character is screwed to a wood base. It has the typical characteristics of the Beer Barrel Blatz man. Notice the white shirt sleeves held in place by garters. This may be an indication of the age of the bank.

The cast iron figure has good molded details, lifelike eyes, a mustache and mouth, wood grain on the barrel, a Blatz Beer label, the hand holding a molded mug with foam, and hair parted in the middle.

Blatz Beer Man — Date unknown
Blatz Brewing Company, 7½", cast iron, $50.00.

BOSCO BEAR & OTHER GLASS BANKS

"Bosco and Milk, The Milky Way to Health!" That was the beginning of a quarter page ad in the December 1942 *Ladies' Home Journal* magazine.

"Wise mothers who know about the 'Milky Way to Health' are serving chocolate-flavored, iron-rich BOSCO AND MILK every day this winter. Some like it hot. Some like it cold. Either way it is nourishing, delicious! Bosco helps your family drink more milk! Milk is one of the most nourishing of all foods. With Bosco added, milk is even more nutritious, more delicious. It's easy for youngsters to drink the quart a day they need."

Pictured with the ad is a black and white illustration of the 1½-pound Bosco Jar, with liquid pouring from it. The label said, "Milk Amplifier/A DELICIOUS CHOCOLATE-MALT FLAVORED SYRUP."

The jar is well marked with "BOSCO" molded into the bottom both vertically and horizontally, crossing at the "S."

Slipped over the plum and white checked lid is a brown plastic bear's head. Around the base "BOSCO BEAR" is molded into the plastic. The molded features of Bosco's eyes and mouth are painted white, lightly sprayed so it looks gray over the brown plastic. The nose and the pupil of the eyes are not painted. Molded separately is a red hat, only an inch high, fitted to the top of Bosco's head. The hat moves and could be slipped off with pressure. In the back of Bosco's head is a slot for coins. The bank is 8" tall.

Other clear glass banks of the 1940's (all food products shown here) were molded subjects. Animals and people fit the zany characters category.

Grapette Products Company of Camden, Arkansas, had a 7½" elephant glass bank. Molded into the bottom: "GRAPETTE/PRODUCTS CO./LG 2597/CAMDEN, ARK."

A Snow Crest Bear bank was marketed by Snow Crest Beverages Inc. The pint bottle was filled with punch flavored concentrated syrup. One part syrup was mixed with six parts ice water. Molded in the bottom of the glass; "PAT PEND MFRD BY SNOW CREST BEVERAGES INC. 17 2 SALEM MASS."

Nash Underwood Inc. of Chicago sold prepared mustard in a 4½" jar, molded in the image of Lucky Joe, a Black character of the era. The 8½-ounce container has ingredients and "LUCKY JOE BANK," the name of the company, printed on the red and white metal lid. Molded in the bottom: "DESIGN PATENT NO. 112688 7."

Bosco Bear — 1940's
Bosco Company,
8", glass and plastic, $15.00.

Elephant — 1940's
Grapette Products Company,
7½", glass, $15.00.

Snow Crest Bear — 1940's
Snow Crest Beverages Inc.,
pint, glass, $15.00.

Lucky Joe — 1940's
Nash Underwood Inc.,
4½", glass, $15.00.

CALIFORNIA RAISIN® & SUN-MAID®

California Raisin & Sun-Maid — 1987
Sun-Maid Growers of California,
CALRAB, Sun-Maid Raisins™,
6" x 6½", vinyl, $25.00.

Actually, there are two zany characters on the California Raisin Bank. The largest character, the anthropomorphic raisin, is a trademark of the California Raisin Advisory Board, adopted in 1986.

The California Raisin Advisory Board or CALRAB, was organized by the California grape growers in 1949 for the purpose of promoting their products. Their most famous trademarks of all time are the California Raisins with their "viney" arms and legs and wrinkled raisin bodies.

In a magazine ad in *Woman's Day*, June 20th, 1989, Ms. California Raisin (8½" tall in her lime green heels) covered most of the page. Her dreamy bedroom eyes are accented with thick black eye lashes and sky blue eye shadow. Hot pink lips seem to be saying, "How wrinkled is Too wrinkled?" The zany character is surrounded with a variety of raisin recipes: Oat'n Orange Muffins with ½ cup of raisins; Asian Salad, only 58 calories; Savory Chicken Pinwheels; and desert...Apple Raisin Oat Crisp.

After the Claymation® figures of the California Raisins, designed by Will Vinton, appeared in animated television commercials, raisin collectibles began appearing on the market. The Sun-Maid California Raisin bank of 1987 was one popular item retailed in chain stores in America.

The other zany character on the bank is the Sun-Maid box of raisins. The Sun-Maid trademark was established in 1915 by the Sun-Maid Growers of California. The words Sun-Maid and the girl with the red bonnet and basket of grapes are printed on the packages of Sun-Maid Raisins.

The bank measures 6" wide and 6½" tall. It is made of molded vinyl. The portion that represents the box of raisins has a red paper wrapper with the Sun-Maid trademarks on it.

A purple raisin man, standing next to the box, has sunglasses, orange tennis shoes, black legs and arms, and white gloves. The box and raisin stand on a yellow base. Markings on the bottom of the bank: "The California Raisins™/®1987 CALRAB/Claymation® designed by Will Vinton/Licensed by Applause-Licensing/Made in China."

CAP'N CRUNCH® & JEAN LAFOOTE®

**Cap'n Crunch & Jean LaFoote — 1975
Quaker Oats Company, 7½",
vinyl, $25.00/$35.00.**

Collectors, keep watching Quaker Oats' Cap'n Crunch cereal boxes! The Quaker Oats Company continues to offer premiums. Two favorite collectibles of the 70's are Cap'n Crunch and Jean LaFoote. In the 1980's two plastic figurines of Cap'n Crunch were included in the packaging. A new Cap'n Crunch doll was available in 1990.

The Cap'n Crunch trademark was adopted about the same time as the pre-sweetened cold cereal bombarded the market in the early 1960's. Cap'n Crunch continues to promote "his" cereal into the 1990's. The old captain, with a long bushy mustache and double chin that drops down to the single gold button on his blue coat, is pictured on every box of Cap'n Crunch cereal. He is also a TV star and has appeared in animated color commercials.

Notice how storytellers include a captain-pirate conflict in the tales of the sea? The same theme was used in the TV commercials. The villain, Jean LaFoote, with sword in hand, tries to steal the precious cargo (Cap'n Crunch cereal of course). Millions of viewers cheer for the Cap'n and hiss and boo the pirate. The animated color commercials were more fun to watch than some of the cartoons! TV viewers young and old alike are familiar with the captain and the pirate.

In 1975, the Quaker Oats company offered Cap'n Crunch and Jean LaFoote 3-D characters in the form of banks. The 7½" plastic banks were sold for $1.50 each and two box tops, barely enough to cover postage and handling.

I suspect more Cap'n Crunch banks were available than the Jean Lafoote banks. In the 1990's Jean Lafoote is much more scarce and expensive.

Cap'n Crunch is made of molded blue plastic with painted features. His face is beige flesh toned and he has white trousers. The gentleman has black boots. The blue hat is trimmed with a gold "C." The jacket, blue also, has gold braid painted on the collar and cuffs.

It is helpful to find marks molded into the plastic such as: "CAP'N CRUNCH®" on the back of the bank. "JEAN LaFOOTE®" is also on the back of the pirate bank. He is recognized by his green suit and purple pirate's hat.

Molded details render both characters as examples of twentieth century plastic art. Notice the facial features, with exaggerated noses and bulging eyes. The pirate has teeth...the captain does not! Belt buckles, buttons, and braid are all included. And to make the characters more appealing to collectors, the coin slots are out of sight!

CHEESASAURUS REX®

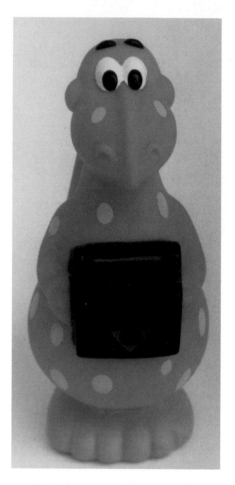

Cheesasaurus Rex — 1992
Kraft General Foods, 7", vinyl, $20.00.

Kraft was established in 1903 by James Lewis Kraft in Chicago. Six years later the company was incorporated and one of many name changes took place. J.L. Kraft & Bros. Co. distributed thirty varieties of cheese under brand names Elkhorn and Kraft.

The company name was changed again in 1928 to Kraft-Phenix Cheese Corporation, when Kraft bought the makers of Philadelphia brand cream cheese. In 1969 the company name changed to Kraftco Corporation and in 1976 it was shortened to Kraft Inc. By 1980 there was another merger and a new name, Dart & Kraft Inc. The 1988 merging with the Phillip Morris Companies Inc. brings us up to date with Kraft General Foods Inc.

J.L. Kraft was notorious for variety in advertising, from the magazine ads to advertising on the elevated trains in the 30's. One of the products given special attention is Kraft Macaroni & Cheese dinners introduced to the public in 1937.

Kraft Macaroni & Cheese dinners remain on the market and J.L Kraft would be proud to see the unique advertising.

Question — How do you entice people to eat more macaroni & cheese? Answer — offer, FREE, the most delightful Brontosaurus ever, to the kids and collectors, when dinosaurs are the fad of the day!

This is exactly what Kraft General Foods Inc. did. A bright gold brontosaurus bank with a treasure chest in his hand was pictured on the box of Kraft Macaroni and Cheese, along with a form. The offer expired December 31, 1993.

Along with the original form, ten UPCs were needed. The larger size box of Kraft Macaroni and Cheese yields two UPCs and the smaller size box has one UPC. Postage and handling for the free premium was $1.00.

The 7" banks are made of gold vinyl in the image of the Kraft General Foods Inc. trademark, the Cheesasaurus Rex. The character has painted eyes and yellow spots. It carries a brown treasure chest. Marks: "©1992 KGF/ CHEESASAURUS REX" embossed on back of body.

CHUCK E. CHEESE® & JASPER T. JOWLS®

"Where A Kid Can Be a Kid®," the slogan of Chuck E. Cheese's pizza parlor, best expresses the company goal and we see it on every ad along with the one of the greatest kid's mascots, Chuck E. Cheese, the famous house mouse.

The reasons they exist, taken from the 1993 McBiz Corporation, (a franchisee of Show Biz Pizza Time Inc.) brochure are as follows:

"We believe that childhood is a magical time to be cherished and enjoyed.

We believe that play is not mere kid's stuff, but rather a crucial part of a child's physical and mental development.

We believe that today, more than ever, families need a safe, wholesome environment in which they can laugh, play, and simply enjoy being together.

We believe that while raising children is a big responsibility, it's also a whole lot of fun. So relax, Mom and Dad, and have a giggle or two on us."

The Chuck E. Cheese pizza houses are the place to go, and have been since the early 1980's, for a total family experience.

Open the doors to a smoke-free environment loaded with activity oriented play areas, games that test skill and the best rides in town. There is even a show about Chuck E. Cheese and his friend Jasper T. Jowls, the banjo playing hound in blue bib overalls and straw hat.

After the fun and games enjoy a Pizza Feast. Before going home, stop at the counter, join Chuck E's Fan Club and receive free tokens. The tokens are used in the same machines. Now is also the time to select the latest collectible of Chuck E. Cheese and Jasper T. Jowls.

The zany character banks were first offered in 1980 for $2.00 each. Some stores continue to carry the banks in the 1990's. If they cannot be found, antique and collectible dealers are asking as much as $15.00 for each bank.

The two characters do not have identifying marks. Chuck E. Cheese is a mouse with a mischievous wink, 6½" tall, standing with one leg crossed over the other, resting on his cane, in front of a large brick of Swiss cheese.

Jasper T. Jowls is one-half inch shorter. The hound leans against a rock wall and has his red banjo under one paw. Both banks are made of molded gray plastic and have painted features.

Chuck E. Cheese — 1980's & 1990's
Pizza Time Theater Inc., 6½", plastic, $15.00.

Jasper T. Jowls — 1980's & 1990's
Pizza Time Theater Inc., 6", plastic, $15.00.

COLONEL SANDERS®

Harland Sanders started a restaurant business in Corbin, Kentucky, in 1930. By 1935 Sanders was recognized for his cooking fame and proclaimed an honorary Colonel by the governor of Kentucky.

Sanders had perfected a chicken recipe and in 1954 he copyrighted "Colonel Sanders Recipe Kentucky Fried Chicken." All the paper products such as napkins, place

**Colonel Harland Sanders —
Kentucky Fried Chicken Corporation**

Left: 1965, Run Starling Plastics Ltd,
12½", plastic, $35.00.
Right: 1977, Margardt Corp.,
8", plastic, $25.00.

mats, barrels, buckets, and cups have the Colonel Sanders image and "It's finger lickin' good!" trademark. When premiums were offered over the counter they also exhibited the trademarks.

Colonel Sanders was 64 and in essence his image became a logo and trademark — an elderly gentleman with a goatee and mustache, wearing a white suit with a black string tie, and carrying a cane.

Kentucky Fried Chicken® was incorporated in 1955 and two years later Colonel Sanders had 400 franchises in the United States and Canada.

The success was wonderful but Colonel Sanders was ready to slow down. He sold the corporation to investors in 1964, who in turn took the company public in 1966. By 1969 Kentucky Fried Chicken was listed in the New York Stock Exchange. Guess who bought the first one hundred shares? The original owner!

There were ownership changes after Colonel Sanders's death in 1980. The Kentucky Fried Chicken Corporation was sold to PepsiCo. Inc. in 1986. There are now 3,000 international Kentucky Fried Chicken restaurants including the huge 500-seat, three-story restaurant in Beijing.

With progress and expansion, changes in products and trademarks followed. Collectors are now hoarding the early advertising and premiums offered by the company.

The 8" plastic bank made in the likeness of Colonel Sanders with a bucket of Kentucky Fried Chicken is one zany character difficult to find. There is no color on the molded Colonel except for the black string tie and the red stripes on the bucket, both are actually a vinyl material.

Details in the molded figure make up for the lack of color. Notice the sculptured effect of the facial features: a well formed nose, indented eyes, the hair lines of the shaped mustache, goatee, and eyebrows.

The Colonel's molded hair is neatly parted on the left side, and combed behind his ears. Five small buttons are molded on the jacket front. The tiny image of the Colonel on the bucket is a surprise! Molded markings on the bottom of the figure: "MARGARDT CORP. 1977®/ P.O. BOX 49282/LOS ANGELES CALIF."

The chicken that comes home for the holidays

Everybody's too busy to fix dinner. Everybody but Colonel Sanders. And he's at work this very day fixing up a feast for you to take home. Finger lickin' good Kentucky Fried Chicken,® piping hot biscuits, gravy, and all the delicious trimmings.

Busy holiday season. Gifts to buy. Presents to wrap. Friends and family dropping by.

No time to cook? Then it's time for you to pick up the

best-tasting, best-selling chicken in the whole wide world.

No other chicken is seasoned with 11 spices and herbs. (According to the Colonel's secret recipe.) And no other chicken is cooked according to his patented process.

There's only *one* Colonel Sanders' Kentucky Fried Chicken. And it's ready to go in minutes from over 1500 locations throughout the country. It's the merriest chicken dinner that ever came home for the holidays.

We fix Sunday dinner seven days a week

Colonel Sanders, ©Kentucky Fried Chicken. *Life*, December 15, 1967.

EVEREADY CAT®

"SAVE WITH THE CAT. ©1981/UNION CARBIDE CORPORATION," are the permanent markings on the Eveready Cat bank. An Eveready 9-volt general purpose sticker is below the slogan.

The "volt," a unit of electrical pressure, was named in honor of Allesandro Volta, the inventor of the first battery in 1798. Volta's battery was of the "wet" type, a rather crude model measured against today's standards.

A German scientist, Carl Gassner, invented the "dry cell" battery in 1888. Two years later, the National Carbon Company began commercial production of batteries. In the meantime, the flashlight or "electric hand torch," as it was called in the 1890's, was invented by a Russian immigrant named Conrad Hubert (born Akiba Horowitz).

The idea developed from an employer's battery-and-bulb device used to light up flowers in a pot. The employer was Joshua Lionel Cowen, the inventor of the Lionel electric trains.

Hubert patented the light and organized the American Eveready Company. In 1914 the National Carbon Company and American Eveready Company merged. The new company was later bought by Union Carbide.

It wasn't until 1956 that the Eveready Company produced the first 9-volt battery.

The Eveready Cat represents the "classic" 9-volt battery. They are easy to identify with a black cat jumping through the number "9" on the silver and red label.

New and better batteries are invented continuously and in 1982 Eveready opened one of the world's largest battery research and development centers in Westlake, Ohio.

The Eveready Battery Company was purchased by the Ralston Purina Company in 1986. The black cat is a trademark of the Eveready Battery Company Inc., now a subsidiary of Ralston Purina Company.

Eveready Cat — 1981
Union Carbide Corporation, Eveready Batteries, 6", plastic, $12.00.

What will life on earth be like in the year 2050? How will scientists solve the energy challenge of diminishing oil supplies and increased electrification? Is the accumulation of carbon dioxide in the atmosphere going to be a problem for our descendants and what method of purification will be used? Will we have the water needed to develop synthetic fuels? In the future, will agriculture technology require more fuel to grow food on less land? What progress will be made in harnessing energy from the sun? What secret energy awaits us in the ocean?

Modern technology in the twentieth century has made unbelievable progress. However, questions remain unanswered and possibilities are undiscovered. If history repeats itself, answers will be found after various options are studied and tried.

To get an insight on the importance of energy and possible changes in the future, travel through time on "traveling theater" cars in the Experimental Prototype Community of Tomorrow (EPCOT), at Walt Disney World near Orlando, Florida.

In this exhibit people are also reminded of how humans have tamed fire, wind, and steam to produce primary sources of energy. Demonstrations on how coal and oil are extracted from the earth and used for energy are shown. In fact, all established sources of energy are reviewed from horsepower to the unsuccessful Three Mile Island nuclear plant. Ideas for the future are presented, such as the peaceful use of nuclear power with commercial fusion reactors that do not create harmful waste products.

What does all this speculation on the energy crisis have to do with Figment, the comical Disney character? Figment is advertising EPCOT. This zany character carries a pot of gold with "EPCOT CENTER" incised in the plastic. Molded into the bottom of the bank: "©1982 WALT DISNEY PRODUCTIONS MADE IN KOREA."

Figment is definitely a figment of the imagination. The body is purple and it has orange wings and horns. The orange pot of gold has a coin slot in the top.

Figment — 1982
EPCOT Center, Walt Disney
Productions©, 6", plastic, $12.00.

GOP ELEPHANT & DEMOCRATIC DONKEY

The new Republican Party was formed July 6, 1854, a few months after the Kansas-Nebraska Bill was passed by the senate. New Republicans opposed the bill, allowing the new territories of Kansas and Nebraska to have slavery if the people there voted for it. Republican goals included gaining office and abolishing slavery entirely.

Republicans, fighting against slavery, absorbed many Whigs, Free Soilers, and Northern Democrats but they were not strong enough to win the presidential election of 1856. Democrat James Buchanan won with 174 electoral votes against Republican John Fremont's 114 votes and the American Party's Millard Filmore's eight votes.

In the meantime Abraham Lincoln, strongly against slavery and once a member of the Whig Party, had joined the Republican Party and paved his way to the Republican convention. In 1860 Lincoln won the presidential nomination for the Republican Party at the convention in Chicago. Consequently he was elected the 16th President of the United States, the first Republican President to hold office.

Succeeding to presidency on Lincoln's death, Andrew Johnson was a member of the Union party. After Johnson's impeachment the Republicans were in office for almost two decades with the victories of Ulysses S. Grant (1868, 1872), Rutherford B. Hayes (1876), and James A. Garfield (1880).

It was during this era that the elephant became a symbol for the Republican Party. Thomas Nast, a popular cartoonist of the 1800's, is believed to be the originator of the symbol, featuring the elephant as the Republican vote, in a political cartoon in one of the 1874 issues of *Harper's Weekly* magazine.

Six years later the Republicans nicknamed their party the Grand Old Party (GOP).

The Elephant, promoting the Republican Party, and the Donkey, promoting the Democratic Party, are popular in the political collectibles field. There are many different versions.

This GOP bank is 3½" tall and 5½" long and made of gray, molded plastic. A GOP sticker covers the coin slot, on the top of the elephant's back. Date unknown.

Marks on donkey, "SAVE YOUR MONEY, YOU'LL NEED IT IF THE REPUBLICANS GET IN!" The ceramic donkey is 6" tall. Marks: "®PAULA 1968, WB# MADE IN U.S.A."

GOP Elephant — Date unknown
Grand Old Party, 3½" x 5", plastic, $10.00.

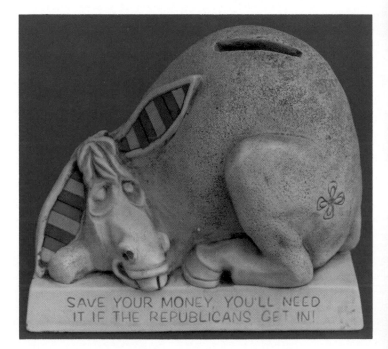

Democratic Donkey — 1968
®Paula, 6", ceramic, $25.00.

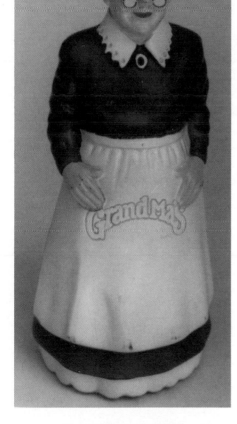

GrandMa — 1970
GrandMa's Cookie Company,
GrandMa's Brand®, 7½", plastic, $30.00.

Have you had any of "GrandMa's" cookies lately? I am speaking of the kind you find at check-out counters and vending machines. You will recognize them instantly by "GrandMa's Brand®" trademark and picture. She is a lovely lady with white hair. Eyeglasses sit low on the bridge of her nose and she wears a white collar over a blue dress.

Currently there are 20 different kinds of GrandMa's cookies with names you won't forget: Peanut Butter Sandwich Creme, The Oatmeal Spice Big Cookie, Candied Animals Snack Cookies and the Fudge Nut Brownie, to mention a few.

GrandMa's Cookie Company was founded by Foster Wheeler in 1914 in Portland, Oregon. It was a family owned company, typical of the times. Foster Wheeler was forced to retire because of poor health in 1942. The company was acquired by Ralph Wittenberg. By 1970, the Wittenberg family had added 40,000 square feet to their bakery and they were selling cookies throughout the Pacific Northwest.

According to a Frito-Lay Inc. brochure, "Marketing Case History," the success of GrandMa's Cookie Company attracted the attention of Frito-Lay, the snack food manufacturing and marketing company. Consequently Frito-Lay purchased the baked goods company from the Wittenbergs on May 20, 1980.

Following a successful test market in Kansas City, Frito-Lay began distributing GrandMa's Brand cookies nationally in 1983. The cookies were no longer confined to the west coast area of Washington and Oregon.

GrandMa became more famous than ever, and like many trademarks, GrandMa took on new dimensions.

The 1970, GrandMa's Brand® character bank has molded and painted features including white hair combed back and tied in a bun, wire rim glasses, a white fancy collar over a blue dress, plus a long white apron with "GrandMa's Brand®" on the front and a ribbon tied in back. The bank is 7½" tall. A slot was made in the back, at shoulder level, for the deposit of coins and a large plug in the bottom for access. Yes, another advertising character with double appeal!

HEATHCLIFF® & HONEY GRAHAM BEAR®

Another type of bank is the plastic product container. Four banks of this type are included in Chapter One. (See NABISCO'S® more sophisticated Mickey Mouse and Donald Duck, 1966 banks.)

Heathcliff Sugar Frosted Flakes® were marketed by Street Kids, Culver, California, in 1988. The container is 13½" tall and made of molded orange plastic. Remove the head to get to the cereal. When the cereal is gone the container serves as a bank. A designated slot in the back is cut open for coins.

Paper stickers represent the eyes and nose. There are no marks on the plastic. A sticker on the back includes ingredients of the cereal, "HEATHCLIFF VITAMIN OFFER," and "Heathcliff Copyright 1988 McNaught Syndicate Inc."

Heathcliff was originally a cartoon character created by George Gately. After Gately had his first major sale to the *Saturday Evening Post*, his cartoons appeared in leading magazines in several countries including Europe, South America, and Canada. *Heathcliff, Triple Threat*, a collection of cartoons, was published by Charter Books, copyright 1976 by McNaught Syndicate Inc. Heathcliff was appearing in newspapers around the world and more collections were published. Street Kids picked up on the popularity of the yellow cartoon cat and sold cereal in a container in the likeness of the zany character.

Street Kids marketed another food product bank in 1990, the Limited Edition Honey Graham Bears Graham Snacks®.

Wouldn't you think with a name seven words long, the cookie might be a whopper also? Wrong…the bite-sized bears are only 1¼" high and about ¾" wide. Look closely and discover details like the pin-dot navel and the tiny toes!

The 10-ounce package of cookies was packed into a plastic container in the image of the Honey Graham Bears. It is made of molded light brown plastic and stands 11" tall. The eyes are paper stickers over molded oval-shaped eyes. There is no indication of feet but at the end of each leg the bear has three shaped toes.

Another label on the back of the bank has an offer for a Graham Bear key ring in exchange for $3.00 and the completed form.

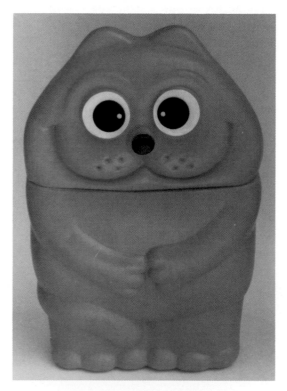

Heathcliff — 1988
Street Kids, ®McNaught Syndicate Inc.,
13½", plastic, $20.00.

Honey Graham Bear — 1990
Street Kids, 11", plastic, $10.00.

Here comes Stormin' Normin followed by Pigsqueak, Chop Sticks, Gloria Vandergilt, and Gater Bait. They are running for the cookies today!

Belly Bust holds the record, 3.51 seconds for 70 feet of U-shaped track. If a pig could run a mile at that speed this would be equivalent to a four-minute mile!

This isn't a fantasy world, this is entertainment and promotion in the mid-west. The Heinold Pig Racing Team was a promotional ploy to advertise the Heinold Hog Markets, based at Kout, Indiana.

The Heinold Pig Racing Team started racing in 1977 at state fairs. They entertained at the 32nd annual Farm Progress Show, northeast of Fisher, Illinois, in 1984 and retired shortly after that.

Roy Holding from Illinois is the man who trained the twenty-nine gilts (virgin pigs) to jump the hurdles and race down a sawdust tract to their reward.

The team traveled from state to state in a 28 foot trailer with running water and fan cooled stalls, "a rolling pig palace" as Holding called it.

Why would a former journalist take on the challenge of training pigs? He wanted to prove swine are not stupid and slow. In four days Holding had the hogs eating out of his hand…they loved the chocolate cookies.

The team of racing pigs were fed a diet of low-fat, high protein hog feed and each season a new team was trained. Pigs have a rather short "prime of life" and when they grew too big, of course they were out of the racing circuit and ready for the Heinold Market!

Another segment of the Heinold promotion was the chuck wagon parked near Heinold Downs, as the race track was named. People could enjoy ham and sausage sandwiches.

Along with all this activity, at the ag-shows the Heinold Company gave out promotional items like small banks. The theme for 1984 was, "It makes dollars and sense to Bank on Heinold Hog Markets."

The 3" banks are bright yellow with a picture of five racing pigs. Black printing marks the banks: "HEINOLD PIG RACING TEAM."

Heinold Racing Pigs — 1984
Heinold Pig Racing Team, 3", plastic, $15.00.

HUSH PUPPIES®

The Hush Puppies trademark is one of the more recent trademarks of Wolverine World Wide Inc., a company founded in 1883 by Fred Hirth and Gustav Adolph (G.A.) Krause, in West Michigan.

Wolverine remained a family concern for many years but it is now a publicly held corporation whose shares are traded on the New York Stock Exchange. The company grew to be an international enterprise with sales of more than $300 million and equity of more than $100 million.

In the beginning, the company's reputation was built on the sturdy farm and work shoes they made from "shell" horsehide. Today Wolverine manufactures and markets a great variety of pigskin leather products as well as more than ten nationally known footwear brands.

The company has conformed to contemporary lifestyles and the footwear products now range from rugged work shoes to high fashion women's shoes. The Hush Puppies brand casual shoes are the company's most famous product.

During the 1950's, research continued on pigskin processing and Victor (son of G.A.) resigned his position as chairman of the board and dedicated full time to researching technology for effective pig skinning methods. At the same time he was testing a new product. He had a pair of shoes made from pigskin and recognized the possibilities.

Why the interest in pigskin? Horsehide supplies were no longer reliable and the cowhide sales were disappointing. There was a tremendous supply of pig skins if only the skinning method could be perfected.

Victor Krause assembled engineers to develop a machine that would separate pigskin from flesh without damaging the skin or decreasing the meat yield. They had a major breakthrough and patented a device that did the job and fit conveniently into the production lines of most packers.

In 1957, the first Hush Puppies shoes were test marketed. The brand was launched nationally in 1958. Hush Puppies brand became one of the most spectacular success stories in the footwear industry.

The famous Hush Puppies logo is a highly recognized symbol for quality footwear around the world.

The trademark evolved from a trip into Tennessee by Jim Muir, the company sales manager. After finishing his fried fish dinner at a customer's house, he asked why the fried corn dough balls were called hush puppies. It seems the fried dough was used by farmers to quiet their barking dogs. Muir reasoned that "Hush Puppies" would be an excellent name for Wolverine's new pigskin shoes because when feet hurt they are much like barking dogs. A brand name was born!

In the 1970's the company used a savings bank in the likeness of the Hush Puppies logo as a sales aid. The brown and tan basset with the sad eyes and long drooping ears is made of molded and painted vinyl. It stands 8" tall. The dog is on a cream colored base. "Hush Puppies® BRAND CASUALS" is molded in the front of the base.

Hush Puppy — 1970
Wolverine World Wide Inc.,
Hush Puppies® Brand Casuals, 8", vinyl, $30.00.

ICEE BEAR®

**Icee Bear — 1974
Icee Corporation,
8", vinyl, $30.00.**

"Icee…Cool, delicious and full of fun!" This was the message from Icee Bear, trademark and logo of the Icee Corporation.

For at least nine years during the 60's and 70's, Icee Bear shared prime time on three major networks with some of the most popular children's programs. The whimsical white bear, in his red sweater, was as entertaining as the cartoons.

The target for the advertising campaigns was children — preschool to pre-teen. Icee Bear was also out there promoting Icee beverages in comic books in a big way.

At right is one of the ads from the September 1977 issue of *Betty & Me*, ®1977 By Close-Up Inc. This isn't a small spot in the bottom of the page, following the romance of Archie and Betty — Icee Bear has no less than a full page! He is holding a cup of Icee® in each hand, with the red fruit-flavored ice, peaked high in each cup. There is no doubt it is Icee® because the cups are the familiar red and blue stripes and have the "ICEE coldest drink in town" trademark.

It is also obvious that Icee Bear is in seventh heaven. He has a big polar bear smile and his eyes are closed as he sips through a straw, in the treat in his left hand.

According to another advertisement, distributed by the Icee Developers Association, Icee Bear was featured in 11 million Marvel Comic Books with 80 titles.

The Icee Corporation also offered premiums and Icee was busy advertising the premiums designed to keep the ice machine busy.

The soft vinyl Icee Bear from 1974 can be either a bank or a squeeze toy. There is a slot in the back to be cut and used for coins. Unusual as it may be, the bank also has a squeaker in the bottom. The double identity no doubt appealed to a greater number of children and collectors.

Icee is sitting and measures 8". He is made of molded vinyl and has painted features. One unusual detail of Icee Bear is his paws. They look like gloved hands with three fingers and a thumb. Icee is a cheerful looking bear with crossed eyes who holds a blue and red cup full of the Icee treat. "ICEE®" is molded in raised letters across the cup. Like the advertising characters, the three dimensional Icee Bear is wearing a red sweater.

**Icee Bear, ©1977 Close-Up Inc.
Betty & Me, September 1977.**

KIRBY KANGAROO® PIGGY BANK

The Kirby Kangaroo Club was founded in 1978 to help credit unions actively involve the youth market, ages 12 and under, in credit union affairs. The program was designed to help children develop good savings habits and perhaps return to the credit union for adult financial needs.

The Kirby Kangaroo Bank, a gold plastic 7" bank, was one of the early premiums, from 1978 to 1984. Marks engraved on the bottom of the bank: "KIRBY KANGAROO® COPYRIGHT 1984 GROUP THREE ADVERTISING™."

The white Kirby Kangaroo Club Piggy Bank, 4" tall and 6" long, replaces the gold bank. "KIRBY KANGAROO® CLUB" is printed on the side and a picture of a kangaroo is included.

Kirby is a busy kangaroo, promoting the children's savings plan through the Kirby Kangaroo Club. We find him on t-shirts and sweatshirts, duffle bags and Bizzy bags, birthday cards and playing cards, fanny packs and purses, and other new items that keep the children interested.

Collectors love Kirby Kangaroo. They can add him to their advertising character and coin bank collections.

Doesn't this sound like fun and games? In reality we are discussing big business. According to the Iowa Credit Union League (ICUL) Services Corporation brochure:

> "Each year children spend a staggering $36 billion in allowance and job earnings, and influence another $48 billion in parental expenditures. In total, kids comprise a market worth $84 billion. And just like adults, kids have money problems…budgeting, saving, spending, and wasting it."

> "Unfortunately, personal finance is rarely taught in schools. At home, only 35 percent of parents discuss money with their children, according to a 1987 Rand Youth poll. While this leaves millions of children at a financial disadvantage, it opens a door of opportunity for credit unions."

Since 1978, ICUL Services Corporation, an affiliate of the Iowa Credit Union League, has provided effective, efficient youth programs to credit unions all across the country. The Kirby Kangaroo Club is designed for the youngest members, 12 and under. This age group is motivated with premium items.

Kirby Kangaroo — 1984
Kirby Kangaroo Club, 7", plastic, $20.00.

Kirby Kangaroo Club Pig — 1994
Kirby Kangaroo Club, 3½", plastic, $10.00.

**Kool-Aid Kid — 1970's
General Foods Corporation,
4½" x 7", plastic, $30.00.**

An artist from Foote, Cone, and Belding, a Chicago agency, "doodled" a smiling face on a frosted pitcher of Kool-Aid and a product symbol was born! The Kool-Aid Kids have represented the Kool-Aid brand soft drink mix since 1953.

Kool-Aid was first distributed by the General Foods Corporation, an old company established in 1895. Skipping much of the company history, General Foods was purchased by Phillip Morris Companies in 1985. Three years later Kraft Inc. merged with the Phillip Morris Companies. As a result of the merger, consumers began seeing a new name on Kraft and General Foods products, Kraft General Foods Inc.

Sales, mergers, and new managers...the Kool-Aid Kids survived it all, now more active than ever. In the 1990's, they continue to dance and make music and participate in a variety of activities in advertising. The animated TV stars have become as popular as any of the cartoon characters.

The Kool-Aid Crowd saves points for "Wacky Warehouse® Free Stuff." What to look for? Yellow one-inch squares printed on all the Kool-Aid products. In the square there is a picture of either the Kool-Aid Kid or a pitcher of Kool-Aid, the words "Proof of Purchase" and the number of points.

Envelopes of Kool-Aid without sugar = one point.
Canisters of Kool-Aid with sugar = twelve points
Sugar Free packages = three points.

Occasionally special promotions are issued like the "Oh Yeah!" cards in canisters of Kool-Aid. The consumer was to call an 800 number and give the card number to receive extra Kool-Aid Points.

The Kool-Aid Kid bank was made in the 1970's. It is the Kool-Aid Kid on a yellow base which holds the coins and measures 4½" by 7".

Information molded in the bottom of the base: "KOOL-AID® IS A REGISTERED TRADEMARK OF GENERAL FOODS AND IS USED WITH ITS PERMISSION. SYNDICATION SERVICES INC. 500 SUMMER STREET, STAMFORD, CONN. 06907 MADE IN HONG KONG."

LINCOLN

The first impression of the Lincoln bust might be — ah-ha!...another Lincoln collectible to add to the Lincoln prints, postcards, photographs, and stereographs.

The metal character has all the traits of the first Republican President (1861–1865). It resembles the much larger sculpture in The Museum of Science and Industry, with wonderful details including minute eyelids, the cleft in the upper lip, hair lines on the chin and head, realistic ears, and the untidy bow tie!

A Lincoln bust may be classified in several collectible fields. Old Abe memorabilia of the twentieth century, Americana, still banks, or zany characters of the ad world!

Printed on the back of Lincoln's shoulders is the following: "LINCOLN/SAVINGS BANK/REINBECK, IOWA/Offices: Lincoln and Dinsdale/Members F.D.I.C."

"A. Lincoln" is engraved in front in script, a duplicate of his autograph perhaps.

How did Abe Lincoln come to represent a bank in a small town in Iowa? The town of Lincoln, located in Lincoln Township in northwest Tama County, was originally called Berlin, a name chosen by the people of German descent that populated the area. The bank in Berlin was first issued a charter by the state of Iowa in June 1902. At that time it was called the German Savings Bank. September 4th, 1902, the new bank was open to the public with $15,000.00 to begin business.

During World War I, our nation fought against Germany and to show their loyalty for the United States, the residents of Berlin, Iowa changed the name to Lincoln. The name corresponded with the township in which the town was located. In May 1918, 40 men (women did not have the right of suffrage) took part in the election. Of the 40, 35 voted for the name change.

Consequently, the stockholders of the German Savings Bank renamed their institution the Lincoln Savings Bank.

The Lincoln Savings Bank survived the depression years by merging banks of four small towns and relocating in Reinbeck, the largest town and centralized location.

Growth was steady during the 50's. In 1960 the bank expanded. At that time the Abe Lincoln still banks were first offered.

The bank celebrated its 90th anniversary in 1992. The Lincoln Savings Bank used the picture of Abe Lincoln as a logo on stationery and advertising and they continue to sell the Lincoln banks. They are made by Danthrico Inc., Chicago, Illinois.

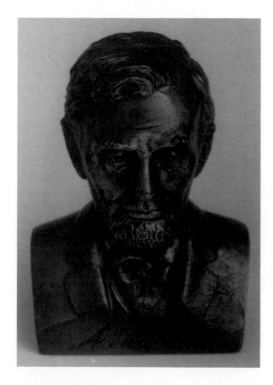

Lincoln — 1960
Lincoln Savings Bank,
5¼", bronze metal, $10.00.

"Look for the RED WHEEL!" In the 1920's and 30's, the Magic Chef stove was referred to as the "gas range with the famous RED WHEEL." Actually the red wheel was a Lorain Heat Regulator, the first thermostatic control to be placed on a gas range.

The homemaker had a new and wonderful modern convenience and with the help of *Magic Chef Cooking*, the days of "burn and learn" were over!

Recipes in *Magic Chef Cooking*, copyright 1924, were tested in the research kitchen of the American Stove Company in Cleveland, Ohio, under the direction of Dorothy E. Shank, a former Instructor of Food Research, Household Arts Department, Teachers College, Columbia University, New York City.

No doubt, the book was good advertising and the American Stove Company believed in advertising. They promoted the Magic Chef stoves as "The New Vogue in Cooking."

Aggressive advertising continued with full page color ads as long as the budget allowed. One ploy was the endorsement of a famous person. In the 1940's they recruited movie star cowboy Roy Rogers to help fight the "range wars." Roy Rogers was featured in "The Old Range Roundup" of 1941. A brand new Magic Chef stove was offered free, to the person who brought in the oldest range.

The image of a chef, as a corporate logo, was invented by the American Stove Company advertising department in 1939. The character in formal attire, including a black bow tie, was included in the ads. One memorable advertisement pictured "Magic Chef" riding a horse. (This was the Roy Rogers ad!) In fact there were three small logos on the bottom of the page, all riding horses!

A short summary of the company chronology includes a name change in 1951. The American Stove Company became Magic Chef Inc. and was then sold to the Dixie Products Company in 1958. In 1960 the company was renamed Magic Chef Inc. Expansion continued with plants in Spain and Italy and new acquisitions such as Admiral and Norge.

At this time Magic Chef Inc. was the fourth largest appliance manufacturer in America. By 1984 sales exceeded $1 billion.

The company was destined to either go ahead or fall back. Nothing ever stands still in the corporate world!

Skeet Rymer of Magic Chef Inc. and Daniel Krumm of the Maytag Corporation began talking about a merger of the two companies. The proposal was approved in March 1986 and Magic Chef Inc. merged with Maytag.

In the 1990's, the Maytag Company now markets appliances under the brand names Magic Chef, Admiral, Norge, and Maytag.

The molded plastic chef, in a black formal suit and chef's hat, was used in Magic Chef promotions. The first 1960's bank, 7½", has "Magic Chef®" molded into the chef's hat.

Magic Chef — 1960's
®Magic Chef Inc., 7½", vinyl, $20.00.

RONALD McDONALD® & GRIMACE®

How did a small hamburger stand, started by two brothers, Maurice and Richard McDonald, in San Bernardino, California, develop into a world-famous restaurant chain? There is no single answer to the question. We realize advertising is certainly one important factor in the success story.

McDonald's Corporation has many advertising symbols and characters. The most noticeable are the huge "Golden Arches" that decorate the skyline along the highways and in cities.

The Ronald McDonald trademark mascot was adopted in 1963, replacing a funny character with a hamburger face by the name of "Speedee."

Ronald, the redheaded clown, is the main advertising character, appearing in all types of advertising from TV to company calendars.

Ronald is a big attraction because he is fun. Kids love him with his friendly, positive personality in a fantasy world driving vehicles of the imagination, enjoying his friends, and exploring.

Ronald premiums have been popular since the first doll offer in 1971. The 7" vinyl bank offered in the 1980's is a favorite collector's item. "Ronald McDonald®" is painted on the base.

Grimace, a big purple fellow, became Ronald's best friend in 1971. Grimace is a happy-go-lucky guy that uses simple words like "uh" and "duh."

Grimace is always asking questions and Ronald, with the patience of a saint, explains and explains. Ronald shows him how to use a skateboard with one foot instead of the two-foot Grimace way! Ronald demonstrates the proper handling of a softball bat...Grimace learns and the children learn.

Grimace, although clumsy and slow, demonstrates optimism and happiness, a good example for everyone.

The Grimace bank is ceramic and stands 9" tall. It is purple and a sticker on the bank reads, "GRIMACE® ©1985 McDonald's Corp. Thailand."

Ronald McDonald — 1980's
McDonald's Corporation,
7", vinyl, $25.00.

Grimace — 1985
McDonald's Corporation,
9", ceramic, $25.00.

"Tie me in, buy me up!" Mickey Mouse and Donald Duck, copyright Walt Disney Productions, are two of the most popular characters licensed for product premiums and have been for some time.

In 1966, NABISCO® retailed a pre-sweetened caramel flavored cereal called Puppets Wheat Puffs®. The Wheat Puffs were marketed in plastic containers, made in the images of Donald Duck and Mickey Mouse. After the cereal was gone, a designated slot in the back of the containers could be cut open and the consumer then had a bank.

It is interesting to note the printing on the lids: "NATIONAL BISCUIT COMPANY, SPECIAL PRODUCTS DIVISION, NEW YORK, NY. MADE IN THE U.S.A., COPYRIGHT 1966 NABISCO."

The National Biscuit Company was the result of New York Biscuit, American Biscuit, and United States Baking companies merging in 1898.

Company history is recorded through the logo. NBC chose to use a symbol composed of an ellipse and a double cross for a logo/trademark. In the beginning, IN-ER-SEAL was printed inside the ellipse. Later, IN-ER-SEAL was replaced with NBC. In 1923 "Uneeda" was added below the seal but by 1935 it was dropped.

The National Biscuit Company replaced NBC with "NABISCO" (the corporate contraction) in 1941. Another obvious change was made when the complete logo was enclosed in a bright red triangle in 1952. The consumers couldn't miss it!

NABISCO continued to add to their company. They acquired Shredded Wheat (1929), Milk Bone (1931), Dromedary (1954), Cream of Wheat (1961), James Welch (candy, 1963), and Standard brands (1981), which consisted of Planters nuts, Blue Bonnet margarine, beer, and wine.

NABISCO became a part of the R.J. Reynolds Tobacco Company in 1985. The company's food and candy processing plants are located throughout the United States, Canada, and Puerto Rico.

"Puppets" are no longer on the market and the character containers are coveted collectibles in the advertising category.

Mickey Mouse, the clown, has the traditional Disney thumb and three-finger hand and "MICKEY MOUSE" molded into the plastic container.

Donald Duck appears ready for a trip to the moon in a white space suit, trimmed in blue and gold. His name is molded into the helmet. The lid on this container has the same printing as the Mickey Mouse.

A copyright notice of Walt Disney Productions is molded on the back of both banks. The banks are 10" tall and made of hard white plastic molded into the shape of the cartoon characters. Features are painted.

Mickey Mouse — 1966 National Biscuit Company, ®Walt Disney Productions, 10", plastic, $20.00.

Donald Duck — 1966 National Biscuit Company, ®Walt Disney Productions, 10", plastic, $20.00.

MOOLA MOOLA®

Question: What has a round magenta head, a green bulbous nose, pink eyelids, three large white teeth and a "happy face" smile? It has no body but it does have hands and feet. There is a coin slot in the back.

Answer: Moola Moola, a make-believe monster from the land of Lotta Loot®!

The zany character Moola Moola represents Moola Moola and the Money Minders®, a savings club for kids, copyright 1983 Bankers Systems Inc.

The club is full of colorful characters designed to teach children good saving habits and have fun too. The Money Minders are Pennyopolop, Doodadime, Two Bits, Scratch, and Nickelodeo.

Moola Club members may purchase bonus items anytime at the regular prices...or they may take advantage of a disciplined savings program and get free prizes.

Here is how the program works. Members receive ten points for making a deposit (maximum ten points per member per week). These bonus points may be used for purchasing prizes at a reduced price...or they may be saved over time to receive any item for free. An accumulation of 100 points yields a FREE Moola Moola Bank, the most expensive prize. The everyday price is $8.00.

Collectors will have no trouble identifying Moola Moola. "MOOLA MOOLA®/MOOLA MOOLA AND THE MONEY MINDERS®/BANKERS SYSTEM INC" is molded into the back of the character.

Moola Moola — 1983
Bankers System Inc., 3½", vinyl, $10.00.

The Chrysler Corporation has the distinction of being the third largest automobile producer in the United States. They sell several vehicles — Chrysler, Dodge, Eagle, Plymouth, Jeep, and Lamborghini.

It began in 1920. The Maxwell Motor Car Company was reorganized by Walter Chrysler. In fact, in 1923 he was the president of the company. A year later Chrysler introduced a new car (named after himself), with a high speed six cylinder engine and overdrive. By 1925 Chrysler took over the Maxwell Car Company and renamed it. Dodge, Desoto, and Plymouth cars were added to the company in 1928.

To learn all about the Chrysler Corporation read Lee Iacocca's autobiography. He became the CEO of the Chrysler Corporation in 1978 and he tells the story. He appeared on TV commercials and continued working after some men his age would have retired.

The Chrysler Corporation diversified into several other businesses: Chrysler Financial Corp., Dollar Rent-A-Car Systems Inc., Snappy Car Rental, Thrifty Rent-A-Car Systems, Maserati, and Mitsubishi.

Mr. Fleet was a Chrysler service man shaped into a bank used in the 70's to promote Chrysler products. Some car dealers gave the character bank to customers as a premium. Mr. Fleet is recognized by the company five point star logo and the name on the shirt. Incised on the bottom of the 9" vinyl bank: "CHRYSLER CORPORATION/1973 MADE IN U.S.A."

Mr. Fleet, a stocky fellow without a neck, has a face the same color as his shirt and belt, an off-white. Bright blue pants and baseball hat are part of the uniform. Shoes and bow tie (a detail that dates a character) are black. A pipe wrench in Mr. Fleet's right hand is gray. Features and clothes are molded and painted.

Mr. Fleet — 1973
Chrysler Corporation,
9", vinyl, $50.00.

Planters Nut and Chocolate Company was started by Amedeo Obici and Mario Peruzzi in 1906. Several years later, they conducted a contest, in search of a logo for their company. The original Peanut man was designed in 1916 by a teenager, Antonio Gentile. A commercial artist took the winning design and added the monocle, cane, and top hat. Mr. Peanut has become an American icon.

Unlike some logos, details keep changing on Mr. Peanut. For instance, the monocle moves from one eye to the other! In a 1918 picture, the monocle is over Mr. Peanut's left eye. A 1927 logo shows the monocle on the right eye. The premium dolls of 1967 and 1970 have monocles on the left eye. The monocle is switched again on the 1993 doll.

On the Limited Edition Planters tin issued in the 1980's, Mr. Peanut is featured 35 times around the bottom of the tin. Sixteen of them have the monocle on the right eye. The others have it on the left!

There are other variations in the logo. Sometimes Mr. Peanut's body has the texture of a true peanut shell. At other times, the texture is eliminated, resulting in a stylized version of a peanut. There is a variety of hats, also. Short hats, tall hats, hats with hat bands, hats without bands.

Look for different faces as well. Mr. Peanut may have realistic eyes, a natural nose, and a human-like mouth with full lips and a friendly smile. Another version is the line drawn features, with a watermelon smile.

Mr. Peanut carries a cane in the logo. The cane may be either a straight stick or a curved handled cane. Thus, when searching for Mr. Peanut collectibles be aware of the many different images. Collectors delight in finding as many versions of the Planters Peanut trademark as possible.

There are several figurals in the shape and form of the peanut man. Salt and pepper shakers in the full figure are highly collectible. Mr. Peanut cups, made in the 1950's, are Mr. Peanut's head and hat only.

The 8½" plastic banks in the likeness of Mr. Peanut are popular. They are made of red, tan, blue, or green plastic. "MR. PEANUT" is molded into the hat band.

A prolific year for Planters premiums was 1992. On the back of one-ounce Planters Peanuts bags, several premiums were offered: a bendable Mr. Peanut ($1.99); a Mr. Peanut mechanical pencil ($2.99); and an 8½" Mr. Peanut bank for $3.99 and three Planters wrappers.

Unlike the early brightly colored banks, these have tan peanut bodies with black arms, legs and hat. The monocle is on the right eye and the cane in the left hand. Mr. Peanut is made of plastic and well marked. Molded into the underside of the base, "MR. PEANUT AND THE MR. PEANUT FIGURE ARE REGISTERED TRADEMARKS OF PLANTERS LIFESAVERS COMPANY/MADE IN CHINA."

Mr. Peanut — 1970's Nabisco Brands Inc., Planters Peanuts, 8½", plastic, $10.00.

Mr. Peanut — 1992 Planters Lifesavers Company, 8½", plastic, $15.00.

"Drink Florida Orange Juice. Florida's standards are the highest — even higher than the federal government's!" How do we know it's Florida's?

We know it's Florida's when we see the "Florida Sunshine Tree®," a symbol found only on 100% pure Florida oranges, grapefruit, and juices.

The symbol is also used extensively in advertising. The first advertising I found in the *Ladies' Home Journal* featuring the Florida Sunshine Tree was in the early 1970's.

In 1986 the State of Florida, Department of Citrus ran a full page, colored ad in women's magazines explaining the Sunshine Tree and they said "The sun shines on our tree up to 355 days a year!" A fruit tree is pictured with oranges *and* grapefruit on it.

The Florida Sunshine Tree trademark resembles a mushroom with a stylized top, composed of fifteen round circles, seven yellow and eight orange. The "oranges" and "grapefruit" are separated with green shapes representing leaves.

How does the Orange Bird fit into the picture? The trademark character was used by the State of Florida, Department of Citrus in the 1970's to promote the sale of the citrus fruits. The Orange Bird Bank was a premium offered.

The Florida Orange Bird is made of plastic and sits, measuring 5". The bird has the texture and shape of an orange. Eyes and beak are molded and painted on the "orange" head. A fantasy type body is added.

Marks include: "FLORIDA/ORANGE BIRD" & "®WALT DISNEY PRODUCTIONS" molded on the back.

Orange Bird — 1970's
State of Florida, Department of Citrus,
®Walt Disney Productions,
5", plastic, $20.00.

PAC-MAN®

OK, I have fed the machine my first quarter and I have the joystick in hand…now press the button to start the game. The "music" begins and four monsters start chasing Pac-Man. Pac-Man is the name of a round character with a wedge cut out for the mouth.

With the joystick I try to control the yellow fellow. We race around the board "eating" dots and dodging the monsters. Shadow, the red monster, follows behind and is always waiting to "eat" Pac-Man at the first chance. Watch out for Speedy, the pink monster. He is faster than the other three! Remember, eat as many of the blue monsters as possible for more points. They may be bashful but beware! And then there is the orange Pokey.

Ah-ha! Listen to Pac-Man "gobble" those dots — wow, I got Bashful! Oops…the machine whines with sympathy as Pac-Man disappears. Speedy caught him!

Another Pac-Man appears and I get a second chance! One minute later and the game is finished. Add a quarter and improve that score, kid!

In the early 80's Pac-Man was the game rage of the decade. Kids of all ages matched their skills in restaurants and casinos betting on Pac-Man. Soon a modified video game of was available for home use and books were published on how to master Pac-Man arcade and home games. Game pro Ken Uston's expert guide tells everything you need to know to keep Pac-Man running and catch the blue Bashfuls and devour everything in the path to accumulate the maximum points.

Although *Mastering PAC-MAN* was neither authorized or endorsed by the Midway Manufacturing Company (owners of the Pac-Man trademark), The New American Library Inc. enjoyed several printings with the first copyright January 1982.

There were other Pac-Man collectibles on the market from toys to yard goods. The bank is made of yellow plastic. Press the orange joystick and the top half lifts and coins may be deposited. The eyes are white with yellow eyelids on a black mask, a one piece sticker placed in the molded eye area. A sticker on the "body" has "TOMY/PAC-MAN®." Molded on the bottom of the bank is "LICENSED FROM AND ® BALLY/MIDWAY, PAC-MAN AND PAC-MAN CHARACTERS™ BALLY/MIDWAY."

The bank is 4" high and the base 2¾" in diameter.

Pac-Man — 1980's
Tomy, ®Bally/Midway, 4", plastic, $25.00.

PIZZA PETE®

Pizza Pete, a comical character with a black mustache, a dust catcher scarf around his neck, an apron and a western hat, was the logo and trademark chosen for Pizza Hut® restaurant services in 1960.

Two brothers, Frank and Dan Carney, college students in Wichita, Kansas, at the time, opened the first Pizza Hut. They hired a cook and a second Pizza Hut was opened in less than a year. By 1971 Pizza Hut was reported as the largest restaurant chain in the world, both in sales and in number of stores.

Pizza Hut Inc. extensively used endorsements in advertising, choosing celebrities to boast about the attributes of "Supreme®," "Pepperoni Lovers®," "Cheese Lovers®," "Meat Lovers®," "Bigfoot®" and all the other Pizza Hut pizzas.

In 1983 the "Personal Pan Pizza®" was introduced and this was a big step in the right direction. Singles on a lunch break could have pizza of their choice in a small portion.

We have not seen Pizza Pete lately but in the 60's he was popular. In fact in 1969 the trademark figure was produced in three-dimensional form. Another plastic bank, a popular premium in the 60's and 70's, was used as a premium. This one was free with a purchase of two large pizzas.

The 7½" bank was designed by a Wichita artist, Ed Pointer. Even with the enormous nose and feet, Pete looks more realistic than the original trademark character. He definitely has the appearance of a satisfied man, with his contented grin and hands resting on a full stomach. The red, white, and blue costume labels Pizza Pete as American (although Pizza Huts are international). Marks include "PIZZA HUT®" molded on the front of the apron.

Pizza Pete — 1969 Pizza Hut®, 7½", plastic, $30.00.

RICE'S PIGGY BANK

"Piggy bank" refers to any small savings bank according to *Webster's New World Dictionary*. A bank in the shape and form of a pig, however, is considered a "piggy bank" by the collectors who hoard the hogs exclusively, as well as the collectors of zany characters of the ad world.

Small plastic pig banks of all colors say "I love New York," "I love Hawaii," "I love Iowa." Some messages are more subtle, like the white ceramic bank with "Something Special, Minnesota." In fact, is there one state that does not advertise on the common pig bank?

Banking institutions are famous for offering pig banks with the name printed on it. Collectors enjoy finding something more interesting like the pink plastic pig that says "Unbelievable Checking, Only From Norwest."

It is the advertiser's ingenuity that intrigues the collector. How do you like this, printed on a wood pig bank: "Pull on my Snoot. Put in the Loot. Wild Bills, Deadwood, South Dakota."

Organizations appeal to the public for funds through piggy banks. Picture a plastic purple pig with the words "They'll Walk, Talk, See. — Elks Major Project."

The Midwestern agriculture companies offer pigs with messages like, "A Growing Part of Your Farm Future, ASGROW."

What could be more suitable for a sausage company than a pig bank? In the 1950's, the R.B. Rice Sausage Company chose a large white plastic pig with a touch of pink. It measures 9" long and 5" tall. Molded on the bank is "RICE'S/PIGGY BANK/R.B. RICE SAUSAGE COMPANY/U.S. INSPECTED/TRADEMARK."

R.B. Rice's Pig — 1950 R.B. Rice Sausage Company, 5" x 9", plastic, $25.00.

SAD DOGGIE

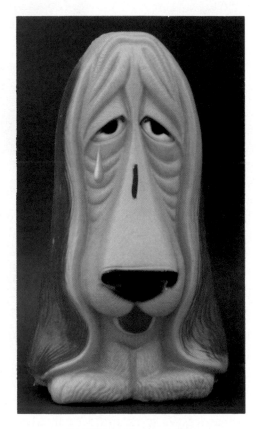

**Sad Doggie — 1980
American Humane Society,
11", plastic, $75.00.**

"I'm so hungry, it makes me cry. If you don't help, I may die."

At least half a dozen yellow dogs were sitting on counters in Wal-Mart, depressed and gloomy, with a tear drop below one eye, and a card stuck in the top of their heads with the above plea for help.

Christmas shoppers hurried from department to department, laden with gifts. Occasionally one would stop and drop a few coins into the slot in "Sad Doggie's" nose.

According to Dale Jamieson from the Animal Rights Association of Jackson, Tennessee, Sad Doggie is America's Number One Collector!

Jamieson said, "Most all Humane Societies are in constant need of funds and over 1,200 societies purchase collection banks from the Animal Rights Association of Jackson."

The Sad Doggie banks are in all 50 United States, four provinces of Canada, the Bahamas, and the Virgin Islands.

The Humane Society began using Sad Doggie in 1983. The banks are placed in fast food restaurants, convenience stores, and other high traffic locations. A "Please Help the Humane Society" card is included with each bank. Donations are collected by the organization and used to support the animal shelters and services that get the animals off the streets.

The American Humane Society was formed in 1877, dedicated to protecting children and animals from human cruelty. The first societies with the same purpose were founded in the 1700's.

The Animal Rights Association of Jackson sells the Number One Collector to Humane Societies exclusively in lots of one dozen or more.

Sad Doggie is 11" tall and about 6" wide. The dog has sculptured hair lines and folds in his skin, well defined eyes and nose. Sad Doggie looks the color of butterscotch candy. A sticker on the bottom says "MADE IN CANADA."

SMOKEY THE BEAR BANK

"Remember, only you can prevent forest fires." Albert Stahl, from the Foote, Cone, and Belding ad agency, designed Smokey Bear as a symbol for forest fire prevention, August 9, 1944, but according to one source the bear was not on the USDA Forest Service posters, with the motto, until 1947.

According to the USDA publication No. 1230, the U.S. Forest Service manages 187 million acres of public land, including 154 national forests and 19 national grasslands in 43 states and Puerto Rico.

The USDA Forest Service also cooperates with state agencies and private owners to stimulate proper management practices and to protect the 440 million acres of their forest against fires, insects, and disease.

Smokey Bear is the official spokesbear for the U.S. Forest Service. We find him educating the children in a variety of media. In the 1950's *THE TRUE STORY OF SMOKEY THE BEAR*, authorized and approved by the USDA, tells the story in a Big Golden Book, and there are many other books. In 1961 Simon & Schuster published a *SMOKEY THE BEAR* stamp book and the same year Peter Pan Records released a 45 rpm record, *SMOKEY THE BEAR*.

Posters are circulated through schools and ranger stations, featuring advice like, "Smokey's Friends Don't Play With Matches," and "Please Be Careful With Fires in the Forest." Smokey is one of our nation's most successful symbols ever and to prove his importance our country celebrated Smokey's 50th birthday beginning October 1993. Officially the celebration continued until August 9, 1994.

Only businesses approved by the U.S.D.A. Forest Service can make and sell Smokey Bear collectibles. Each item is also approved before it can be marketed. Smokey Bear dolls, statuettes, and banks must resemble the logo according to specifications.

Royalties from sales of Smokey Bear merchandise are collected by the Forest Service and used to help prevent forest fires.

Our Smokey the Bear bank may not be licensed by the U.S.D.A. Forest Service. It is 14" tall, made of brown plastic. Painted features include a yellow hat and belt buckle with "SMOKEY" incised on each, a green base and blue trousers. A spade and sign are molded with the bear.

Incised in the bottom of the base is "SMOKEY THE BEAR 1972 ©PLAY PAL PLASTICS, INC."

Smokey the Bear — 1972
©Play Pal Plastics Inc.,
14", plastic, $55.00.

"Good Grief!" Snoopy is up to his old tricks, sleeping on his doghouse roof. The roof isn't just Snoopy's resting place. One time he wrote a novel with his typewriter on the roof. After the novel was published where did he go to read the reviews? On the doghouse roof!

All of this happened in 1971 in *Snoopy and "It Was A Dark And Stormy Night,"* by Charles Monroe Schultz.

Why is Snoopy writing on top of the doghouse? No doubt the roof is symbolic of the author's private place — free from doorbells and telephones.

Schultz was born in Minneapolis, Minnesota, in 1922. He liked to draw cartoons but it wasn't until the late 1940's that his cartoons were recognized and published by newspapers and magazines.

Schultz started the famous "Peanuts" comic in 1950. The Peanuts Gang includes Charlie Brown, the round faced character with an almost bald head and beady eyes, Lucy, and the dog Snoopy. There are others in the gang. You know how social groups are, members come and go. Some of the other names we see are Charlie Brown's teacher, Miss Othmar, and classmates, Peppermint Patty and Pig-Pen!

Schultz often portrays his characters in life situations. He reveals the humorous side that isn't always appreciated.

Charlie Brown is portrayed as a loser but in reality he and the rest of the Peanuts Gang are anything but losers. "Peanuts" comics appear in more than 2,000 newspapers in about 70 countries.

The increasing popularity of the black-eared beagle has made Snoopy one of the most sought after, licensed characters in history. Some of the foods endorsed by the Peanuts Gang include "Snoopy's Original Ice Cream & Cookie Co.®" opened on Fisherman's Wharf in San Francisco, California, in 1984. Tourists could stroll the boardwalks with "Beagle Brownies®" and the "Peanuts Classic®" (chocolate ice cream with peanut butter and chocolate covered peanuts).

Have you noticed Ralston's Whole Grain Wheat Chex®, Rice Chex, and Corn Chex? They all exhibit the Peanuts Gang. Who could resist a box of Ralston cereal with a red plastic Snoopy bank taped to the top? Snoopy is lying on his doghouse. It measures 7" x 4". Snoopy is painted white and has black ears.

Markings include "©1958, 1966 UNITED FEATURES SYNDICATE, INC.," printed black letters on the lower back of the doghouse. Molded in the bottom near the coin access, "MADE IN CHINA."

Snoopy — 1980's
Ralston's Whole Grain Wheat Chex,
©United Features Syndicate Inc.,
4" x 7", plastic, $5.00.

I have before me, *The Amazing SPIDER-MAN, The Web Closes!* authored by Stan (the man) Lee and illustrated by Jim (madman) Mooney…"Marvel Tales" published by the Marvel Comics Group, copyright 1974 and a reprint, courtesy of Non-Pareil Publishing Corporation, copyright 1965.

Spider-Man is hanging from the ceiling behind a bedroom door. He says, "It's Gwendy! Boy…she must have taken a double dose of pretty pills today!"

Spider-Man waits for Gwendy to leave her father's room. Spider-Man had a conversation with the old gentleman. After that Spider-Man has an hour of wearisome "web-slinging." His "spider sense" is tingling! He is getting closer to his destination as he crawls up and down the high rise buildings.

Eventually Spider-Man "shoots his web" to save a beautiful blond from an undesirable character…and in the end he takes off his blue and red costume and reveals his identity as young and handsome Peter Parker.

Spider-Man continues to be popular with the younger generation and when a cereal company had the spidey-sense to tape a Spider-Man bank to the cereal box, you can bet the shelves were cleared before a spider could shoot its web!

The Spider-Man bank was a premium in 1991. It is a 6¾" red plastic, molded figure of Spider-Man from the waist up. Spider-Man's arms are folded in front of his chest. The spider-web lines in the red costume are molded into the plastic but they are not black as those of the comic book character. A spider image is molded into the back of the bank. There is also the recycling symbol and "HDPE" molded below the spider. Paper stickers cover the eyes. A black paper spider is glued to the chest. The belt is blue.

Markings on the back of the paper belt: "Manufactured by STREET KIDS/Los Angeles, CA 90016/Copyright 1991/Marvel Entertainment Group Inc./All Rights Reserved."

Spider-Man — 1991
Street Kids, ©Marvel Entertainment
Group Inc., 6¾", plastic, $5.00.

TAPED CRUSADER

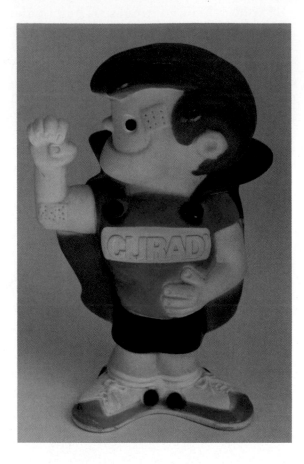

Taped Crusader — 1975
Kendall-Futuro Company,
7½", vinyl, $25.00.

In 1993 the Kendall-Futuro Company, a division of the Kendall Company offered a "New! Stays on Longer," and "Ouchless" Curad®.

The "Value Pack" contains 70 assorted sterile strips; 15 1", 35 ¾", and 20 snips. (Snips are for the tiny injuries and measures ⅜" x 1⅝".) These Curad sheer strips are packaged in a white plastic reusable container.

Another sign of the times is the triangle symbol indicating the packaging is a product from recycled materials.

Some of us remember when the containers were made of tin and the Taped Crusader was a zany character of the advertising world. The boy appeared to be Curad's best customer.

In the 1970's a molded vinyl bank in the image of the Taped Crusader was offered on the package at a cost of $1.50. The features and clothes are painted. In addition to the clothing, the rough and tumble Crusader has a bandage on his left temple, right arm and left leg. Look closely and it appears as though the Taped Crusader needs another bandage below his right eye to cover a triple scratch.

The Taped Crusader is 7½" tall. The designers had collectors in mind when they made this bank. The coin slot is on the head but not visible when looking straight at the character. Special attention was given to details. Close examination reveals minute fingernails, pin point ventilation holes in the "Curad" bandages, and tiny eyelets with laced shoe strings in the sports shoes. Notice the style lines in the boy's hair and the tiny buttons on the cape.

The Taped Crusader has the features of the stereotyped "bully" with a large protruding chin and thin mouth. His thick hair is russet, the same color as the cape. He wears black knee-length shorts and a green T-shirt. The shoes are painted the same green with white.

Identifying marks include, "CURAD" molded on the shirt and painted blue. In the back of the boy, down near the heels of the shoes, incised in the vinyl: "TAPED CRUSADER ©1975 Promotional Marketing Corp."

**Tony the Tiger® — 1962
Kellogg Company, 8½", plastic, $40.00.**

"Kellogg's Frosted Flakes®. They're GR-R-Reat!" Just ask Tony the Tiger®, the robust trademark character on the front of every box of Kellogg's Frosted Flakes® cereal since 1953.

There are many different tigers used for promotional purposes by other companies but there is no mistaking Kellogg's Tony® with his caricature features of a well-fed tiger. Most Kellogg Tony the Tiger® characters have a red scarf with "Tony" printed on it.

The 8½" vinyl bank was offered in 1962, on the Kellogg's Frosted Flakes® box. The bank was free with box top and coupon.

Tony® may appear to be a happy-go-lucky tiger with nothing more to do than entertain the kids while they watch the TV commercials and smile at them at the breakfast table, but in reality he has an important job. If this tiger had an official job description, it might read like this:

Tony the Tiger®, Professional Persuader. Objectives:

1. Convince the public a cold breakfast cereal is as good to eat as hot cereal. They have added vitamins in Kellogg's Frosted Flakes®.
2. Remind the public that cold cereals are quick and easy to fix. Children can make breakfast without any help!
3. Sell them on the idea that Frosted Flakes® are great for parties too. They add flavor and texture to homemade treats.
4. Become a household name on the tip of everyone's tongue and subtly invade the domestic caves of kids and collectors in the form of premiums like banks, dolls, and radios.

UNCLE SAM

How did the personified symbol of the United States with the familiar costume of stars and stripes originate? There are conflicting ideas but the original idea is credited to Samuel Wilson.

The town of Arlington, Massachusetts, claims Uncle Sam was born there. They have placed "Uncle Sam's" monument on the corner of Massachusetts Avenue and Mystic Street, very near the site where Samuel Wilson was born September 13, 1766.

Samuel Wilson left Arlington when he was nineteen. Many years later he had a meat packing business in Troy, New York, and it was his company that provided meat to the United States troops during the War of 1812.

The meat was packed in barrels and the barrels were stamped U.S. As the story goes, many people asked what the U.S. stood for. They were told the letters stood for Uncle Sam!

Uncle Sam again appeared in the book *The Adventures of Uncle Sam*, in 1816 and cartoons in the 1830's.

In 1961 congress passed a resolution, saluting Samuel Wilson as the person who inspired America's national symbol.

Uncle Sam became one of the most popular pitchmen in the nation. Advertisers use the image to promote anything and everything...after all if it's good enough for Uncle Sam it's good enough for anyone. One of the most famous posters is Uncle Sam coaxing the young men to join the armed forces. In an early twentieth century ad, Uncle Sam smokes a pipe and holds Union Leader Cut Plug. Uncle Sam has served as a logo for companies such as Oshkosh B'Gosh Inc. in Oshkosh, Wisconsin, and Blake's Lotsaburgers Inc. in Albuquerque, New Mexico.

Variations appear in the costume Uncle Sam wears but you can be sure it will include striped trousers and a swallow-tail coat. The tall top-hat always has a band of stars. His vest may be blue, or blue with white stars. It may be red or red and white striped. The patriotic colors are indicative of the Uncle Sam personification.

During the Bicentennial of the United States, Uncle Sam was a favorite subject for premiums and advertising. The 11" Uncle Sam bank is made of hard plastic, with molded features and clothes. Uncle Sam has a white top hat with a blue band and white stars. He wears a white shirt and red bow tie. The swallow-tail coat, vest and star studded cape are painted a bright blue.

Products intended for retail or premiums, to celebrate the 200th birthday of the United States, were manufactured at least a year ahead of time. Molded into the base of Uncle Sam: "COPYRIGHT® ALL STATES MANAGEMENT CORP. 1974" and "®UNDER UCC ALL STATES MANAGEMENT CORP. 1975."

Uncle Sam — 1976
Copyright All States Management Corporation, 11", plastic, $45.00.

**U.S. Mail Carrier — 1991
U.S. Postal System, ®Huron Products
Company, 10", vinyl, $15.00.**

Sometimes I find zany characters in the most unlikely places. I went to the post office during the Christmas season of 1991, to do what everyone with the habit of sending Christmas cards does at that time of the year…buy more stamps. When I left the office I not only had stamps, I had postcard puzzles, "Love" stamp earrings, a Christmas stamp pin, and the U.S. Mail Carrier bank in the shape of a mouse!

Not all post offices had collectibles for sale. The district manager said the U.S. Mail Carrier banks were only available in Iowa and Illinois post offices and only 300 were sold to customers. The U.S. Mail Carriers may prove to be highly collectible. There were so few and they fall into several categories — banks, promotional items, and U.S. postal collectibles.

Originally male and female U.S. Mail carriers were available. The male mouse has a light blue shirt and dark blue pants, and the female mouse has a dark blue skirt with the same shirt. The clothes are glued to the 10" vinyl characters.

Although at first glance an observer may perceive them as another "Mickey Mouse," they definitely are not. The molded features include a tuft of hair on the forehead, exaggerated cheeks, two front teeth, big oval eyes, and a round nose.

Add the mail pouch with the U.S. Mail registered trademark and there is no doubt as to who this character is. There are other marks: "Huron Products Co." embossed under the right foot and the back of the neck.

The letter in the pouch serves as a reminder of how the elaborate U.S. postal system began. In 1639 the General Court of Massachusetts established the first postal system. All the mail that came from overseas was to be left with Richard Fairbanks at his house in Boston. Fairbanks was given a penny for each delivered letter.

On July 26, 1775, Benjamin Franklin was chosen by the Continental Congress to be Postmaster General of the American postal system. However, according to the "letter" it was not until 1789 that Congress, under the Constitution of the United States, approved a Postal Service. At this time the country already had 75 local post offices. Stamps were first sold to the public on July 1, 1847, in New York City.

The practice of offering collectibles, other than stamps and books on stamps, over the U.S. Post Office counter was discontinued after 1991.

OTHER BANKS TO LOOK FOR

Benjamin Franklin — Date unknown
Copyright Huron, Almanac, 9", vinyl, $35.00.

Bart Simpson™ — 1990
Matt Groening®, ©20th Century
Fox F.C., 9", vinyl, $15.00.

(See information on Simpsons™
in Chapters Two and Four.)

Cabbage Patch Kid® — 1983
Original Appalachian Artworks Inc. copyright, 6½", vinyl, $20.00.
(See information on Cabbage Patch Kids in Chapter Two.)

CHAPTER TWO

Promotional Figurines & Bendies

ARBY'S® CHARACTERS

"Different is Good!" Just ask Arby's restaurant. Their advertising and cups carry the message. "How to be different? Let Arby's count the ways — 'Beef 'n' Cheddar, Potato Cakes, Jamocha Shakes.'"

Arby's, the fast food chain specializing in hamburgers, was acquired by Royal Crown in 1970. During the 70's and early 80's Arby's kid's meals included the delightful characters from the series of Mr. Men™ and Little Miss™ books written by Roger Hargreaves. Each figurine has "HARGREAVES LIC. BY NEA," and the date molded into the bottom of the feet.

The characters are made of vinyl and measure 1½"–2". The figures have small hands and feet providing balance, enabling the characters to be free standing.

Mr. Men™ and Little Miss™ characters are shaped to show their obvious personalities. Mr. Tickle is orange; he stretches his arms to abnormal lengths and holds on to a tiny blue hat. The smiling, yellow Mr. Bounce has a red molded baseball cap. The green character with a very long nose is appropriately named Mr. Nosey. And poor blue Mr. Bump is wrapped in bandages — even his thumb — because he can't help bumping into everything.

Mr. Mischief is yellow with a blue nose, squinty eyes, and a red hat. Mr. Strong has a red square body and a green hat. Mr. Funny, with a yellow top hat and a wide black mouth, makes everyone laugh. The blue cloud figure is Mr. Daydream.

Five Little Miss™ characters from the 1980's are shown here. The avocado-colored character with bright orange hair and a wristwatch is Little Miss Late. Little Miss Sunshine is bright yellow and has pigtails with red ribbons. Lilac-colored Little Miss Naughty, with a bright green ribbon, has no hair but continues to have a happy face. Little Miss Shy has straight black hair and is blue. She shyly holds her hands over her mouth and blushes like a school girl. And last is Little Miss Trouble, blessed with brilliant orange hair and an abundant crop of freckles. She looks very mischievous with her hands over her mouth, suppressing a laugh.

Chesapeake Financial Corporation acquired Royal Crown and all its divisions, including Arby's, in 1984.

Mr. Men™ Characters — 1971 Hargreaves Lic. By NEA, Manufactured for Arby's Restaurants, 1½"–2", plastic, $3.00 each. Mr. Tickle, Mr. Bounce, Mr. Nosey, and Mr. Bump.

Mr. Men™ Characters — 1972–1978 Hargreaves Lic. By NEA, Manufactured for Arby's Restaurants, 1½"–2", plastic, $3.00 each. Mr. Mischief, Mr. Strong, Mr. Funny, and Mr. Daydream.

Little Miss™ Characters — 1980's Hargreaves Lic. By NEA, Manufactured for Arby's Restaurants, 1½"–2", plastic, $3.00 each. Little Miss Late, Little Miss Sunshine, Little Miss Naughty, Little Miss Shy, and Little Miss Trouble.

"Aye, caramba...don't have a cow man." It's called "smart talk" when it comes from the mouth of second grader Bart Simpson. Teachers, parents, and children were tuning in on the TV series to see what Bart was up to next. The older generation raised eyebrows and snickered in private. The youngsters laughed and giggled and often identified with the obnoxious character. In one episode, Bart had to stay after school and write on the blackboard, "I will not call my teacher Hot Cakes."

If fame had a name in 1990, it would be Bartholomew J. Simpson, the creation of cartoonist Matt Groening. The public was literally bombarded with the Simpsons, mostly Bart. This weird and wired wonder-boy made the front cover of *Time, Entertainment Weekly,* and *Sunday Register TV and Cable Guide.* And who was it that danced across the silver screen promoting Butterfinger candy bars as though he were a real live person and ate the candy bars every chance he got? Bart Simpson!

Everywhere you went, t-shirts exhibited Bart and his quotes — the most controversial, perhaps, "Underachiever and Proud of it."

Bart was anything but an underachiever, with TV series, albums, and videos. It is not surprising that toy companies began making characters resembling Bart and his family, trademarks belonging to Matt Groening and Fox.

When all this was going on, the Burger King® Corporation began sharing the spotlight with the Simpsons. Advertised in animated TV commercials, exclusive Burger King Simpson dolls were available for five weeks. Each week a new doll was offered. They were $3.49 each with a purchase of either blueberry muffins or fries. (See Simpson dolls on page 113.)

Later in the season a set of five PVC Simpson characters on a camping trip were offered. Homer and Marge are 3½" tall. The family members are 3" tall.

Homer holds an orange sock that he has taken out of his boot. A skunk sits on the boot.

Marge appears to be bird watching with a bird book under her arm and binoculars in one hand. Perhaps she doesn't see the birds...there are six in her beehive hair style!

Bart is loaded with all the comforts of home. His backpack includes a TV and skateboard.

Lisa took her sax along and a rabbit has found a new hiding place.

Baby Maggie makes herself at home; with pacifier in her mouth, she stands on a sad looking turtle!

All characters are marked "TCFFC, MADE IN CHINA, ™1990," molded in bottom. Marks on plastic bag with each character "MANUFACTURED FOR BURGER KING CORPORATION."

Simpson Family — 1990
Matt Groening copyright, Twentieth Century Fox®,
Manufactured for Burger King Corporation, 3" to 3½", PVC, set of five $15.00.

CALIFORNIA RAISINS® (GENERAL FOODS)

The years 1988 to 1990 may be recorded in advertising history as the time of the "raisin ruckus." In 1988 the California Raisins with purple, wrinkled bodies and black stick legs debuted on TV. They danced to the tune of "I Heard It Through The Grape Vine." It was a "grape" hit and was named the Best Television Commercial of the Year.

Those were the years the public was bombarded with grape facts and figures such as: How many grapes does it take to make one pound of raisins? (about 4 pounds). What is the California Raisins' birthplace? (Fresno, California). How old are the California Raisins? (Old enough to have wrinkles, but young enough to rock 'n' roll).

Believe it or not, the California Raisins had their own Raisin Hot Line Number — a convenient 800 directory listing for anyone that wanted to know anything about the raisins!

General Foods Corporation was behind all this activity in the promotion for Post Natural Raisin Bran.

California Raisin characters were pictured on the cereal boxes, spooning the raisins into a bowl of bran flakes. On the back of the box all the "free stuff" was featured. They offered two different sets of California Raisins resembling the animated TV characters. The first offer expired September 30, 1989. They were not exactly free. The consumer was asked to send in two proofs-of-purchase and $4.95 for the set of four, 2½" plastic figures. The first set included a saxophone player and three singers. One holds a microphone, another wears orange sunglasses and tennis shoes and a third has blue tennis shoes. The California Raisin characters have white gloves. Licensed figures are marked on the bottom of the feet with date and "CALRAB" (California Raisin Advisory Board).

The second offer expired September 1990. The four California Raisin characters were free with six UPCs or two UPCS and $3.99. There is a drummer, a tambourine player, a singer and a violinist.

California Raisins — 1988 ©General Foods, California Raisin Advisory Board®, 2½", PVC, set of four $20.00.

California Raisins — 1989 ©General Foods, California Raisin Advisory Board®, 2½", PVC, set of four $20.00.

California Raisins. ©1989 CALRAB, Post® Natural Raisin Bran, General Foods Corporation.

CALIFORNIA RAISINS® (HARDEE'S®)

From 1987 to 1991 Hardee's fast foods capitalized on the popularity of the California Raisin trademark characters. They enticed children and collectors to their eating establishments with promotional figures.

The plastic toys are only 2" tall and have all the charm of a plump raisin with stick arms and legs.

The first set offered are The Musicians. Notice the eyes: three of the four musicians have their eye lids squeezed tightly shut, as they sing into a microphone, and play a saxophone and trumpet. The fourth one is different. He has sleepy blue eyes accented with lavender lids and holds his hands up near his ears.

The second set offered in July and August of 1988 are The Stunts. They are equipped with roller skates, a skateboard, a surfboard, and a "boom box." The character on roller skates has a yellow baseball hat with an orange "H" on it. All features, equipment, and clothing are molded and painted. Oh yes, the eyes...two have the same sleepy eyes with lavender lids and two are wearing sunglasses.

In December 1988 Hardee's offered California Raisins again. It was a Christmas promotion and this time the toys were made of polyester fiber and stood 5"

tall. There are four different toys. The soft Raisins were still available in January of 1989. They sold for $2.19 a piece and no purchase was required.

In 1991 Hardee's had a California Raisin promotion again, the "Limited Edition Series," a set of four plastic California Raisins the same size as the first two sets. The major difference on three of them was the elaborate hair styles.

Hardee's promotions are dictated by the management of the individual restaurants. These promotions are not a national or international activity.

Printed on the cards that came in the package with the toys was: "Hardee's, Meet the Family of the 90's" and other exciting information. Ben-Inda-Sun (the bald one) has finally settled down and left the road of musical madness behind. "Benny" has a wife and two kids and enjoys the good life. His wife Anita Break, a working woman and shopper extraordinaire makes her last stop of the day at Hardee's..."Nothing but the best for her family!" Buster, Benny's No. 1 son, is Fresno's "secretary of skate" and the daughter Alotta Style is "simply the sweetest thing on the vine."

California Raisins, Musicians — 1988
©Hardee's, California Raisin Advisory Board®, 2", PVC, set of four $20.00.

California Raisins, The Stunts — 1988
©Hardee's, California Raisin Advisory Board®, 2", PVC, set of four $20.00.

California Raisins, Christmas — 1988
©Hardee's, California Raisins Advisory Board®, 5", plush, set of four $8.00.

California Raisins, Limited Edition Series — 1991
©Hardee's, California Raisin Advisory Board®, 2", PVC, set of four $20.00.

CAMPBELL KIDS® 1994 FIGURINES

In January, a cheerful, red haired, Campbell Kid dressed in his birthday suit and a Campbell's ribbon, burst into the "Souper New Year" with the following jingle:

"We're greeting 1994
With this souper holiday cheer:
Here's to all our loyal friends,
Good health throughout the year!"

The Campbell Soup Company started the new year with a beautiful color calendar, featuring Campbell Kids artwork recreated from Campbell Soup Company archives circa 1920.

The inside cover features a brief history of the Campbell Soup Company started in 1869 by Joseph Campbell and Abram Anderson.

A major milestone occurred in 1897, when a young chemist, Dr. J.T. Dorrance, joined the firm and literally took the water out of soup. The new condensed version reduced expenses to the extent that the company could offer a 10½ ounce can of soup for 10¢ at that time. Many facts that enter into the success of the company are noted. For instance, in the beginning the Campbell Soup Company advertised 21 different kinds of soup and now, after 125 years, there are more than 120 different soups.

Included with the calendar was the "special edition collectibles" order form. People could send for "souper" magnets, cookbooks, tins, a wood Campbell's Soup case, mug set, and horses pulling a Campbell's Soup wagon. All required Campbell's Soup labels with cash.

The calendar was only the beginning of 125th anniversary commemoratives. Later in the season the Campbell Soup Company offered 4" porcelain figures of the Campbell Kids for $6.99 and two Campbell Soup labels for each set. The first set is a boy holding a crate of Campbell's Soup and a girl holding a dish of Campbell's Soup.

The second offer features two Campbell Kid chefs, one black and one white. Each has the identifying "C" on the hat.

Dick Edmiston is the artist that keeps the Campbell Kids forever young. He joined the Campbell Soup Company in 1971 as a designer and illustrator and he keeps a tradition alive that started when Teddy Roosevelt was president.

Campbell Kids — 1994
Campbell Soup Company®, 4", porcelain, $10.00 each.

Cheesasaurus Rex — 1991
Kraft Inc.®, 5", vinyl, $10.00.

The first dinosaur offer from Kraft Inc. was in 1991. It was a 5" vinyl character, available with five proofs of purchase from boxes of Kraft Macaroni &

Cheese, and postage. Actually there were four different characters available: a baseball player, surfer, snorkler and a skater.

This was a short term promotion offered in June that expired in September. The mail-in offer was in the Sunday paper advertising supplements.

In June 1992, there was a new offer in the Sunday papers. This time it was the same Cheesasaurus Rex but, you may have guessed, it was one of the Dream Team, a basketball player on his way to Barcelona, Spain!

The vinyl bendable character has molded and painted clothes and features. It is dressed in a white T-shirt and shorts trimmed with blue. A red and blue "USA" is on the front. The shoes are red and white.

The Olympic Dinosaur offer expired September 30, 1992 and required proofs-of-purchase from six packages of Kraft® Macaroni & Cheese Dinners: Original, Family Size, Dinomac, Teddy Bears, Wild Wheels, or Spirals.

Kraft advertised that they are official sponsors of the U.S. Olympic Team and "Kraft sets the U.S.A. Olympic Training Table."

DINO®

Dino — 1991
Hanna-Barbera Productions Inc.®, 2½" to 3", vinyl, $2.00 each.

More dinosaurs! It must be due to the never ending attraction of dinosaurs for the younger generation that we experience this dinosaur population explosion.

The General Foods Corporation has joined the bandwagon. "Now you can get all three awesome

DINO™ Sports Figures Free. Check out Dino's skateboard style, his rad rollerskating, his awesome skiing moves! To get your FREE set of DINO™ Sports Figures send in two proofs-of-purchase from any Post® Dino Pebbles, Fruity Pebbles®, or Cocoa Pebbles® cereal boxes and $1.00 for shipping and handling, with the order form printed below," (printed on the cereal boxes).

Collectors are warned the supply is going fast and they should HURRY. In small print we find the offer expires August 31, 1993, or until supply is gone.

There were two methods of getting the three Dinos. Fill in the order form and send the required proofs and postage or keep buying cereal until you have all three figures.

These sports figures are hot-pink vinyl characters with painted features. They have happy faces and minimum clothes — vest and hats molded with the character. They stand 2½"–3" tall.

"Dino" and "Pebbles" are registered trademarks of Hanna-Barbera Productions Incorporated.

Marks on the figures "H.B.P. INC© 1991 USA."

DISNEY AFTERNOON FIGURINES®

The Kellogg Company strayed from their company trademark premium trend in 1993. What we saw on the back of Frosted Flakes® cereal boxes, instead of a Tony the Tiger® premium, was a collection of colorful Disney Afternoon figures, the Darkwing Duck® series. Consumers were instructed to check local TV listings and watch "Darkwing Duck," and send for the four vinyl figurines, free with one order form and one proof-of-purchase.

More Disney Afternoon figures were offered on the back of the large box of Kellogg's Rice Krispies®. The "Goof Troop®" was available for one order form and two proofs-of-purchase. This set of hounds, Pete, Goofy, Max, and PJ, were also free.

There were several participating cereals in the Kellogg "Collector's Edition" figurine offer. The collector could have all 16 Disney TV figurines in exchange for six proofs-of-purchase and $1.15 postage and handling.

The UPC symbols could be cut from any of the following Kellogg cereals: Froot Loops®, Rice Krispies®, Frosted Flakes®, Cocoa Krispies®, Corn Pops®, Apple Jacks®, Smacks®, Fruity Marshmallow Krispies®, and Frosted Krispies®. The offer expired October 31, 1993.

The "Collector's Edition" includes The Duck Tales® — Uncle Scrooge with his bag of money, the little girl Webby, Louie, and Gizmo; The Rescue Rangers® — Chip & Dale, Monterey Jack and Gadget; The Gummi Bears® — Gruffi, Tummi, Cubbi, and Sunni. The last four are the Tail Spins® — Baloo, Molly, Don Karnage, and Kit.

The assortment of colorful characters range in size from 1½" to 2½". Most of them have "Kellogg's Co." embossed on the bottom of one foot. "Disney, China" and "1992" are also embossed on the bottom of the feet.

Disney Afternoon Figurines (Courtesy of Kellogg Co.) — 1993
Kellogg Co., Walt Disney Productions®, 1½"–2½", vinyl, $2.00 each.

Darkwing Duck Series: Darkwing Duck, Gosalyn, Launch Pad McQuack, Mega Volt.

Goof Troop: Pete, Goofy, Max, PJ

The Duck Tales:
Uncle Scrooge,
Webby, Louie,
Gizmo.

Rescue Rangers:
Chip & Dale, Monterey Jack, Gadget.

Gummi Bears: Gruffi,
Tummi, Cubbi, Sunni.

Tale Spins: Kit, Molly,
Don Karnage, & Baloo.

THE DOMINO'S NOID™

In the 1980's everyone who enjoyed pizza was trying to avoid the Noid (trademark of Domino's Pizza). The Noid was the character blamed for all the undesirable traits of a pizza gone bad! Because of the Noid the consumer was often standing in line hours at a time waiting for pizza, or the pizza sat on the shelf, soggy, cold and forgotten before it was delivered. The Noid danced around a pizza, in his red devilish suit, trying his best to wreck the popular pies.

There was one sure way the consumer could avoid the Noid. We were reminded on the TV commercials, in flyers, and other advertising: "Call Domino's Pizza. The NOID can't ruin our hot, delicious pizza, because Domino's Pizza avoids the NOID. We hand-make each pizza exactly as you've ordered it, and you get fast, free delivery of our quality pizza in less than 30 minutes."

The Noid Claymation® was designed by Will Vinton Productions Incorporated. Vinyl bendy characters were promotions at Domino's Pizza parlors. They have molded marks including the date and "DOMINO'S PIZZA."

Noid characters were available in several sizes, 2½", 4½", and larger.

The latest Domino commercials feature new stars, Donny and Dottie, domino-like bendable characters, with rectangle bodies, black with white dots and "stick" arms and legs.

These two characters are in the TV commercials and on the large posters. I predict they will soon be offered over the counter, just as the Noid was.

The Noid™ — 1980's
Domino's Pizza®, vinyl, 2½"–4½", $3.00–$5.00.

AVOID THE NOID™   CALL DOMINO'S PIZZA®

When you want pizza, you have to watch out for the NOID.™ He's always out there, ready to ruin your pizza. Sometimes he makes you wait too long for your pizza, or he makes your pizza cold or soggy. What can you do to avoid the NOID?

Call Domino's Pizza. The NOID™ can't ruin our hot, delicious pizza, because Domino's Pizza avoids the NOID. We hand-make each pizza exactly as you've ordered it, and you get Fast, Free Delivery™ of our quality pizza in less than 30 minutes.

DOMINO'S PIZZA DELIVERS® FREE.

©1986 Domino's Pizza, Inc. Litho in U.S.A.

One call does it all!®

The Noid™, ©1986 Domino's Pizza Inc.®

ELSIE®

Elsie — 1993
Borden Company®, 3½", PVC, $10.00.

"Guess who's on the mooove?" It's Elsie the Borden cow and the public is sure to know it with all the new advertising in the 1990's, from billboards to TV commercials.

Although the advertising is new, the Jersey cow, trademark of the Borden Company, is anything but new. Elsie was an essential part of Borden's advertising as early as 1936 and she has appeared on a variety of collectibles. In the 1940's Elsie was popular on postcards, games, puzzles, and recipe books.

Borden's isn't the first company to search into the past and revive a famous trademark. People 30 and over recognize the beautiful bovine with the daisies around her neck in an instant.

It is interesting how the professional persuaders have updated the Elsie image with fresh flowers and short "perky" horns. She wears a sparkling white bib apron with "Elsie's Market" printed on it. The apron covers a blue, or green, or purple blouse.

Elsie's children, Beulah and Beauregard, have taken on new names, Bea and Beaumister. (I don't know where Beaumister fits in the 1990's image!) Both have the latest pop-culture toys, the headphones and skateboard.

TV commercials feature the whole family complete with Elmer, Elsie's husband. (You know, Elmer from Borden Elmer's Glue.)

Elsie is busy promoting the twentieth century products in all the right places.

A full page, colored ad in *Weight Watchers* magazine features Elsie serving the new "Lite Line" lunch.

"Take two slices of lite bread, add your favorite garden vegetables, some honey mustard and slices of delicious Lite Line. Garnish with fresh fruit."

Lite Line is a dieter's dream. It has only 25 calories per slice and no fat. According to Elsie's Market Shopper's Circular this is Elsie's favorite lunch in 1993.

In another advertisement in a Sunday supplement Elsie is promoting both regular and fat-free cheese in a singles keeper. On the bottom of the page we see a modern Elsie with a red shirt and blue jeans.

Collectors could get a free bendable toy in exchange for three UPCs from Borden Singles Cheese Products. The bendable Elsie toy figurine is 3½" high. The offer expired December 31, 1993.

Remember, "If it's Borden, it's got to be good."

Elsie. ©Borden Inc., 1993.

HOLLYROCK TOYS®

HollyRock Toys — 1992
Hanna-Barbera Productions Inc.®,
3" to 4", vinyl, $5.00 each.

Yabbadabbadoo, family fun for you! Hanna-Barbera Productions Incorporated added a new dimension to family entertainment when they created Fred and

Wilma Flintstone and pals Barney and Betty Rubble. The Flintstones first appeared on TV in September of 1960. They lived in Bedrock City, 345 Stone Cave Road with their daughter Pebbles and their pet Dino.

In the 90's several companies gave the Flintstone comic characters as premiums. General Foods offered them on the Post® cereal boxes. The "Holly-Rock Toy" offer expired December 31, 1993. The FREE premium offer required a small charge of $1.15 for postage and handling.

Fred, Barney, and Dino have taken over Holly-Rock. Their features are molded and painted and the bottom of the feet embossed markings read, "©1992 H-B PROD. INC./LIC. H-B PROD. INC./MADE IN CHINA." Dino the Producer is 4" tall and has a magenta body and a yellow shirt. He carries a "TAKE 1" sign. Barney the Cameraman is 3½" tall, wears a green shirt and violet shorts. Fred the Director is 3⅞" tall, and has an orange shirt and blue shorts.

KOOL-AID® MAN FIGURINES

Kraft General Foods Inc. had more collectibles in 1993 than ever before. Consumer could find "Wacky Warehouse Free Stuff" order forms at the point of sales early in the year.

The promotions were drawing attention to Kool-Aid Koolers® and bottled Kool-Aid-Burst® in all the latest flavors including "Pink Swimmingo.®" For 205 points a consumer could have a Kool-Aid Burst punching bag. It is the shape of the Kool-Aid Burst bottle. The travel radio is the same shape and required 240 points. Red plastic Kool-Aid pitchers with the happy face were available for 85 points and the cups to match were only 20 points each.

Trolls By Russ and Mattel's Barbie doll with clothing marked with Kool-Aid logos were also available. (See Chapter Four.) Some people will want them all. Selective collectors may save points for the trademark characters only. The "Kool-Aid Man" figurines required 12 points and 90¢ postage and handling each. There was a choice of a basketball player, a tennis player, and a weight lifter. They are 2" tall and made of hard plastic.

These characters resemble the Kool-Aid guys on the TV commercials, personified red pitchers with molded and painted features. "KRAFT GENERAL FOODS CHINA" is embossed on one foot.

Kool-Aid Men — 1993
Kraft General Foods®,
2", hard plastic, $3.00 each.

McDONALD'S® AND BARBIE®

Collectors of McDonaldland® ad characters and premiums will notice a definite pattern in the promotional plan. The first premiums involved trademark characters belonging to the McDonald's Corporation including Ronald McDonald®, Grimace®, Birdie®, and Big Mac®.

In 1988 we see Ronald and a new McDonald's trademark character, Mac Tonight®. Some are cruising in jeeps, cars, or motorcycles.

The 1990's is the era of cross merchandising with licensing agreements. Marketing miracle workers came up with the unique idea of offering miniature replicas of the original 11½" fashion dolls made by Mattel Inc.® The figurines are made of hard vinyl with molded and painted clothes and features. All are 4" – 5" tall. The first set has molded hair. In the second set the figurines have hair that can be styled.

All are marked on the bottom of the characters "Made for McDonald's® 1992 Mattel Inc./Made in China."

The first 1992 set of Barbie figurines include the following eight: "Snap 'n Play Barbie" wears a playsuit with a bright orange top and green shorts. A second outfit can be snapped over the first. The blond Barbie is then wearing a plastic pink and lavender dress.

"Sun Sensation Barbie" wears a gold bathing suit with an aqua cape.

"Rappin' Rockin' Barbie" swivels at the waist and has a black hat, jacket, and skirt. The shirt and boots are pink. This doll also has blond hair.

"Roller Blade Barbie" of course has pink skates and there are rollers under the base so she can move.

"Birthday Surprise" wears a delicate peach gown and ribbon in her brunette hair.

Another blond doll, "Rose Bride Barbie" wears a white wedding dress with pink roses and beads.

"My First Ballerina Barbie" is a beautiful brunette dressed in blue. She dances the day away as she moves on the swivel base.

Blond "Sparkle Eyes Barbie" wears a long, three tiered shimmering party gown.

The second set of eight Barbie figurines have heads more like the original Barbie dolls. They swivel at the neck and have "hair you can style."

"Birthday Party Barbie" is a black doll with black hair and has a white dress with pink and blue "frosting" stripes.

"Twinkle Lights Barbie" has blond hair and a long dress with a white bodice and pink skirt.

"Secret Hearts Barbie," going out to a Valentine's Day party, has blond hair, a white dress with red trim and a red heart shaped box of candy.

"Romantic Bride Barbie" is also blond. The white bridal gown is trimmed with peach ribbon and flowers and has a textured net overlay.

"Paint & Dazzle Barbie" is dressed in a hot pink mini-skirt, jacket, tank top, and has hot pink heels.

"Western Stampin Barbie," dressed and ready for the American line dance craze, has blue boots, jacket and hat. The skirt is a silver gray.

"Hollywood Hair Barbie" has the longest blond hair ever and she sports metallic gold boots, skirt and jacket.

"My First Ballerina," a white doll with brown hair, dances in white tights under a purple and white costume.

The 1992 Barbie figurines offered with McDonald's "Happy Meals®" are trademarks owned by and used under license from Mattel Inc. Collectors want, but can't always find, the original bags the figurines come in. The bags include dolls' names and copyright information. There is also a pamphlet with coupons and pictures of new Mattel products.

See photos on the next four pages.

McDonald's Restaurant — 1980's
McDonald's Corporation®, Fisher-Price (division of Quaker Oats Co.)

Mac Tonight — 1988
McDonald's Corp.®,
3", plastic, $3.00.

Mac Tonight characters with vehicle — 1988
McDonald's Corp.®, 2"–3", plastic, $3.00 each.

Ronald & glow-in-the-dark star — 1988
McDonald's Corp.®, 3", PVC & plastic, $12.00.

Ronald in car & Grimace — 1990
McDonald's Corp.®, 2"–2½", vinyl, $3.00 each.

Birdie, Big Mac, Grimace & Ronald cars — 1980's
McDonald's Corp.®, 2", plastic, $3.00 each.

McDonald's® Barbie® Dolls — 1992
Made for McDonald's®, 1992 Mattel Inc.®, 4"–5", plastic, $5.00 each.

MOLDED HAIR BARBIE DOLLS

Snap 'n Play Barbie, Sun Sensation Barbie, Rappin Rockin Barbie, Roller Blade Barbie

Birthday Surprise Barbie, Rose Bride Barbie, My First Ballerina Barbie, Sparkle Eyes Barbie

"HAIR YOU CAN STYLE" BARBIE DOLLS

Birthday Party Barbie, Twinkle Lights Barbie, Secret Hearts Barbie, Romantic Bride Barbie

Paint & Dazzle Barbie, Western Stampin Barbie, Hollywood Hair Barbie, My First Ballerina Barbie

"Mirror, mirror on the wall, who is the fairest of us all?" And the mirror replied, "Her lips blood red, her hair like night, her skin like snow, her name — Snow White!"

Grimm's Fairy Tales, written in 1812 by two brothers, Jacob and Wilhelm Grimm, is basically German history, mythology, nature and fantasy. In the last, 1857 edition, there were 210 tales. Many of the classics remain children's favorite stories into the next generation.

Snow White and the Seven Dwarfs were immortalized in Walt Disney's first, full length animated feature in 1937. It was done in technicolor and the addition of songs like "Whistle While you Work" and "Heigh-ho, Heigh-ho" give it special meaning. The original played a total of five weeks at Radio City Music Hall in New York City.

Although Walt, or Elias Disney, born in 1901, died in December 1966, his genius for entertainment lives on. New generations continue to have the opportunity to see *Snow White and the Seven Dwarfs* as young parents introduce the stories they grew up with to their children. The youngsters know and love the beautiful Snow White, the dashing Prince and the seven Dwarf friends.

What happens when McDonald's Corporation makes a deal with the Walt Disney Company to offer figurines of characters in the Snow White classic to customers? The kids of the new generation are thrilled and for eight weeks straight, they flock to McDonaldland to get their favorite characters in the Happy Meals®. They want them all! If they neglect a week they will discover it is very difficult to get the character they missed. And if they don't go early in the week they will find the supply is gone before they get there. (This is the voice of experience!)

Each week a new plastic figurine is offered — Snow White and the wishing well; the Queen that transforms into the wicked witch; a charming Prince and his white horse; Doc with the huge diamond in his mining cart; Dopey and Sneezy together on a swivel base; Happy and Grumpy on a hand car; Sleepy who falls asleep when the arms are moved; and Bashful hiding in the cart of jewels. They measure 2½"–4" tall.

The 1992 characters have two copyrights, McDonald's Corporation and The Walt Disney Company. "®DISNEY" is on each character.

Snow White and the Seven Dwarfs® — 1992 Walt Disney Company®, McDonald's Corporation, 2½"–4", plastic, $5.00 each.

The Wicked Witch & Snow White

The Prince

Doc & Bashful

Happy & Grumpy

Dopey, Sneezy & Sleepy

McDONALD'S® CABBAGE PATCH KIDS®

"We will not sell our babies! (You have to adopt them.)" What an ingenious approach to marketing! Xavier Roberts retailed, pardon me, adopted out the Little People® faster than they were born, in the late 1970's.

The Little People are totally original, soft sculptured, one-of-a-kind babies, boys and girls. Some of them have birthmarks, freckles, dimples, and occasionally diaper rash!

Roberts constructed the Little People from four-way stretch, polyester knit fabric and they were all given an abundance of yarn hair in any of seven different colors. The eyes are hand painted. When they are fully developed, they measure 23"–24" and the birth weight is between 2 and 3 pounds.

The Little People were adopted out of "Babyland General," in Cleveland, Georgia. When they left the hospital an official Birth Certificate, recording the name, birth date, measurements and footprints, was given to the new parents.

Little People were a big hit and Xavier Roberts became famous. The story is, the adoption waiting list was long and Roberts couldn't keep up with adoption applications. After much thought and discussion a new doll was offered for adoption, The Cabbage Patch Kids, ®1982 Original Appalachian Artworks Inc. manufactured by Coleco Industries Inc.

The head and the price are the most obvious differences between the entirely handcrafted Little People and the new Cabbage Patch Kids. The Cabbage Patch Kids have a vinyl head with rooted yarn hair. The Cabbage Patch Kids were readily available for adoption because of assembly line production.

Books on the Cabbage Patch Kids followed such as *The Shyest Kid in the Patch* and *Making Friends* published by Parker Brothers.

Ten years after the Cabbage Patch Kids first hit the market, some of the McDonald's restaurants offered miniature Cabbage Patch Kids as premiums. They are 3¼"–3½" tall. The hair is molded and additional strands of yarn added for the ponytails. The vinyl dolls have heads that move. A couple swivel at the waist and the arms move. The features and clothes are molded. Five CPKs were offered: a Kid in a hot pink nightgown; an angel; a birthday party CPK with a violet dress and a green present in one hand; a ballerina with lavender bodice and tights; and a Christmas Kid in a green skirt and red sweater.

The markings "CPK" and "®1992 O.A.A" (Original Appalachian Artworks) are molded into each doll.

In 1989 Hasbro Inc., acquired the Cabbage Patch Kids from Coleco Inc. a company no longer in business.

Cabbage Patch Kids — 1992
Original Appalachian Art Works®, McDonald's Corporation,
3¼"–3½", plastic, $5.00 each.

Mickey Mouse, a trademark of the Walt Disney Company, was created in 1928 and the cheerful mouse has appeared on a multitude of various items that have become collectible.

The popularity of the Mickey Mouse cartoon character was and still is an inspiration to toy manufacturers and companies who offer premiums with their product.

There are people that collect Mickey Mouse exclusively. They find him in the form of squeak toys, banks, and dolls of all sizes. Old toys and cartoons demand exorbitant prices.

In the June 1992 issue of *Antiques & Collecting*, it was reported that the rare cel painting of Mickey Mouse from his sixteenth cartoon, "Just Mickey," released in the early 1930's, sold at the Howard Lowery's auction of art from American animated films for $19,800!

Collector's News featured a 1931, lithographed tin, Mickey Mouse jazz drummer toy made by Nifty Toys.

This Mickey had four fingers and a thumb. It was only 7" tall and sold for $4,000 at the James Julia Auctions in Fairfield, Maine.

I mentioned the four fingers and thumb because the Mickey Mouse designed by Disney has only three fingers and a thumb. According to Ralph and Terry Kovel, early Mickey toys were made in Europe from sketches of Mickey, and they had the extra finger.

The bendable Mickey Mouse figure was a subscription premium offered in the June 1992 issue of the *Mickey Mouse Magazine*. The magazine is published four times a year by Welsh Publishing Inc., copyright the Walt Disney Company.

"For $12.17 receive five issues of *Mickey Mouse Magazine* and the 5" vinyl toy." Mickey has painted and molded features. Marks: "©DISNEY/MADE IN CHINA" embossed on the bottom of one foot.

Mickey Mouse — 1992
Walt Disney Company®, 5", vinyl, $10.00.

NABISCO® BENDIES

The Sprinkled Chips Ahoy Party Kid® is definitely one I would not have wanted to miss! It is not only a trademark character but it fits into a second category, a "pop culture collectible," a mixture of razzmatazz and vinyl!

Take a good look at the Party Kid. The bendable figure has a face like a chocolate chip cookie sprinkled with rice-like candies. A pair of blue sunglasses rest on a chocolate chip nose. His painted clothes are hot pink print shorts and a pink and white baseball cap to match. White tennies with orange stripes are tied with green shoelaces.

Would a kid dressed like this stand out in a crowd? No way...that's the style these days! We call it classless fashion...one size fits all! Blue jeans are another example of "classless" fashion. They show up everywhere from campus to the White House. Call it advanced capitalism, culture of the free, or American arrogance.

The Party Kid is symbolic of the 1990's. It represents the "new age," not a plain, ordinary chocolate chip cookie but one with razzle-dazzle!

To get the free, 5" plastic toy collectors needed a mail-in certificate from a package of Sprinkled Chips Ahoy Real Chocolate Chip Cookies®, one brand seal from the package and $1.49 for handling and postage. Offer expired March 31, 1993.

The Sprinkled Chips Ahoy Party Kid bendy is made in the image of NABISCO® Sprinkled Chips Ahoy Real Chocolate Chip Cookies. It's the company's "spokescookie," advertised as being ready for party time anytime!

Oreo Cookies, introduced in 1912, are also honored with a namesake. The 4½" bendy resembles the chocolate sandwich cookie with the thick and creamy filling. Frosting squeezed out of the top serves as the "hair" on the character. "OREO®" raised molding marks the back of the cookie and "CHINA" is on the bottom of the right foot.

Sprinkled Chips Ahoy Party Kid & Oreo — 1990's
NABISCO®, 5" & 4½", vinyl, $5.00–$10.00 each.

"Tang, the taste your mouth can't wait for!" Tang is a trademark of General Foods Corporation and the Tang Trio Claymation® was designed by Will Vinton Productions Incorporated.

A card was included with each character. Let me tell you about Lance, the leader, the one showing his muscles. Some call him "Hot Lips." They say, when it comes to smooth-talking nobody comes close to the magic Lance can lay down. His friends call him "King of Cool" and follow his every word. He was the first to discover that mouths could actually leave their faces and he is the only lip known to lips who can smooth-talk and sip a Tang juice box at the same time!

Now Awesome Annie, the one with the yellow bow, is world renowned Lip-Sync Champion. She is fast on her lips. She is so good you can't tell when she is lip-syncing or when she is speaking in her own voice. Her favorite saying is "Sync or Die" because she will never back down from a challenge. According to the card, her greatest achievement was to lip-sync eight songs, skateboard, moonwalk, and chew gum at the same time.

She is now creating her own video, co-staring with Flap the Rapper. They stop only long enough to rest their lips and fuel up on an ice cold Tang juice box.

The characters in the Tang Trio are 2" tall, made of vinyl and stand on their own two feet. Their clothes and features are painted. Lance has a brown shirt, black shoes and blue pants. Flap has a gray shirt, blue pants and orange shoes. Annie has a bright pink blouse with yellow, white and blue dots. The ribbon, legs and arms are banana yellow. The shoes are the same color as the lips.

Embossed in the vinyl of the bottom of the feet, "TANG™/©GENERAL FOODS," and "MFG APPLAUSE INC/CHINA."

Hardee's offered The Tang Trio over the counter at a discount in January 1990. They were 89¢ each with a purchase of food.

Tang Trio — 1990
Tang™/© General Foods, 2", vinyl, $3.00 each.

WENDY'S®

**Wendy® & Good Stuff Gang® — 1985
Wendy's International Inc., ®H.W,
2¼", plastic, $3.00 each.**

**Alf® — 1990
Wendy's, Alien Productions®,
3½", vinyl, $3.00 each.**

R. David Thomas opened the first Wendy's restaurant in 1969. He named the restaurant after his daughter, and the little blond girl with the pigtails became the trademark.

Wendy's restaurants specialized in cooked-to-order hamburgers in the beginning and later some of the foods added were chicken, baked potatoes, a salad bar, breakfast menus, and buffet.

The company began franchising in 1972 and trained managers how to operate a Wendy's restaurant and maintain the image of the company. By 1978 there were over 1400 Wendy's restaurants and franchises. In the 1990's there are Wendy's restaurants and franchises in 22 countries other than the United States.

Advertising on TV produced unbelievable results. Remember the brassy little lady going up to the counter and demanding, "Where's The Beef?" Clara Peller became more famous than Wendy after that debut! She was a part of an $8 million advertising campaign in 1983.

Some Wendy's restaurants used a premium plan. Like their competitors, McDonald's and Burger King, they offered toys with a purchase. In 1985 a red plastic, 2¼", figure of Wendy, a pink figure of Over Stuffed®, and a blue figure of Sweet Stuff® were offered. Embossed on the base of each is their name. Embossed on the bottom of each is the following: "Wendy® and The Good Stuff Gang®/AVAILABLE EXCLUSIVELY AT WENDY'S, ™ & ©1985 H.W., ©1985 WENDY'S INTER'L. INC."

In the late 1980's children had become familiar with the many faces of Alf through books printed by Checkerboard Press: *Alf, Mission to Mars, A Day at the Fair, Summer Camp Adventure,* and *The Great Alfonso.*

By 1990 everyone knew who Alf was and Wendy's offered six 3½" vinyl characters in the likeness of Alf, as premiums. Marks on the bottom of each character: "© ®1990 ALIEN PROD., ©1990, WENDY'S/MADE IN CHINA."

CHAPTER THREE

Miscellaneous Advertising Characters

AVON'S® BETSY ROSS

"Avon Calling!" The direct-sales, one-on-one contact with the customer has made Avon a household word. Avon was reported as the fourth largest retailer of cosmetics in 1989 with $1.6 billion in U.S. sales and $1.7 billion in foreign countries.

Where did it all begin? David McConnell, a New York salesman in the 1880's, gave housewives a small bottle of perfume for giving him the opportunity to show his books. As the legend goes, the women were more interested in the perfume than the books and with this knowledge, McConnell developed the California Perfume Company.

Evidently it was his idea to let the ladies do the selling. Showing is always more successful than telling and they were and still are walking, talking examples of how Avon makeup could transform women into "you never looked so good" customers.

In 1929 the California Perfume Company was renamed Avon and ten years later it became Avon Products Inc.

Avon now has direct sales of costume jewelry, fashions, fragrances, makeup, educational toys, skin care products, gift items, and videos. They also retail "Giorgio," "Oscar de la Renta," "Perry Ellis" "Red by Giorgio" and "Uninhibited by Cher."

Avon Products Inc. is famous for unique bottles. It would require a small warehouse to store the entire line of bottles offered by Avon. Most collectors select a category that interests them and are happy with a cupboard full of Avon decanters in the shape of characters, cars, or whatever.

Antique collectors may ignore the modern and search for bottles made when the company was the California Perfume Company, before 1929.

Collectors of zany characters of the ad world recognize Betsy Ross as another advertising character. The bottle was filled with 4 ounces of Topaze cologne, and sold by Avon during America's 200th birthday.

Anything and everything made to celebrate the bicentennial of the United States is collectible. We have here a bottle with "JULY 4 1976" molded into the bottom.

The glass is painted white with the colors of the flag painted over the front of the skirt. A hard plastic figurine, in the image of Betsy Ross from the waist up serves as the ornamental lid.

The following is printed on the sticker on the bottom of the bottle, "AVON/BETSY ROSS/FIGURINE/TOPAZE COLOGNE."

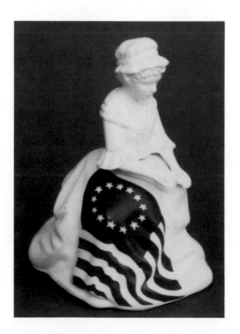

Betsy Ross — 1976
Avon Products Inc., 5½", glass & plastic, $12.00.

It appears advertising played a major part in the success of Avon Products Inc. The Peanuts Gang® was licensed by Avon to endorse products.

Snoopy endorsed Avon's non-tear shampoo. Eight ounces of shampoo was in a red plastic bottle in the shape of Snoopy's doghouse. The doghouse is 3" high and 4½" tall. The lid is covered with Snoopy standing in front. Marks molded into bottom of doghouse: "AVON/SNOOPY & DOGHOUSE/Non-Tear Shampoo AVON PRODUCTS INC., N.Y., N.Y 10020/®UNITED FEATURES 1969."

Snoopy helped sell aftershave too. The Snoopy bottle is white glass with black plastic ears and a blue plastic baseball cap over the lid. The dog is sitting and measures 6". Marks on paper sticker: "AVON/Snoopy/EXCALIBUR/AFTER-SHAVE/5FL. OZ./AVON PRODUCTS INC./NEW YORK, N.Y. 10020/United Features/1969."

Avon also used Charlie Brown and Lucy. The 6", white plastic characters have molded and painted features. Charlie has a red shirt and black trousers, Lucy a red dress trimmed in white. Lids on the bottles served as hats.

Markings molded into the plastic: "AVON LUCY BUB-BLE BATH, AVON PRODUCTS INC./®UNITED FEA-TURE 1952" and "AVON CHARLIE BROWN Non-Tear Shampoo/AVON PRODUCTS, INC. N.Y., N.Y. 10020 4FL OZ/®UNITED FEATURES 1950."

Snoopy & Doghouse — Copyright 1969 United Features®, Avon Products Inc., 3" x 4½", plastic, $10.00.

Charlie & Lucy — Copyright 1950 United Features®, Avon Products Inc., 6", plastic, $10.00 each.

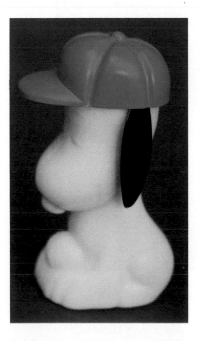

Snoopy — Copyright 1969 United Features®, Avon Products Inc., 6", glass, $15.00.

BUBBLE BATH CHARACTERS

The "contour" bottles of the 80's and 90's are much more sophisticated than the "Soakies®" of the 60's but like the plastic bottles of thirty some years past, these also contain the substance of relaxation and the remedy for rebellion at bath time.

The images of bubble bath characters continue to follow the fads and fancies of the day, from new monsters in movies to the classics. Here are some I have found:

The 8½", red plastic Blockhead™ bottle was made in the U.S.A., distributed by M & L Creative Packaging, Ontario, CA. It has a paper sticker with painted facial features. Marks on sticker on the back "©1987 Prema-Toy Co. Inc."

Comic book heroes the Teenage Mutant Ninja Turtles® of 1984 became TV stars by 1988. They were originally designed by Kevin Eastman and Peter Laird.

The Bubble Bath Turtles are 9½" tall, made of plastic and distributed by DuCair Bioessence a division of Tsumura Int'l Inc. Molded and painted features include "L" (for Leonardo) on the belt buckle.

The copyright date 1989 and "MIRAGE STUDIOS" is molded into the base. Other turtles to look for are Michelangelo, Donatello, and Raphael.

Another bottle is the Jurassic Park™ Dinosaur. Quoting from the tag, "If it's not Jurassic Park it's extinct." In the early 1990's a wave of official Jurassic Park products and licensed promotional items were on the market, as the result of the success of the movie *Jurassic Park* based on the novel by Michael Crichton. Marks molded into the bottom of the recycled 9½" plastic bottle: "JURASSIC PARK™ & ©1992 U.C.S & AMBLIN ENTERTAINMENT INC. (U.C.S. is Universal City Studios Inc.) BOTTLE MADE IN CHINA/DIST BY COSRICH DIV. OF PMC INC./PERTH, AMBOY, NJ 08861."

**Blockhead — 1987
Prema-Toy Co.,
8½", plastic, $10.00.**

**Leonardo — 1989
Teenage Mutant Ninja Turtles,
Mirage Studios®, Tsumura Int'l Inc.,
9½", plastic, $10.00.**

**Jurassic Park Dinosaur — 1992
Universal City Studios &
Amblin Entertainment Inc.®,
Cosrich Div. of PMC Inc.,
9½", plastic, $10.00.**

Cookie Monster® was originally designed by Jim Henson in 1954 as part of the "Muppet®" crowd. The Muppets are stars of Sesame Street (®Children's Television Workshop), and Little Golden Books (®Western Publishing Company Inc.). They have also starred in *The Muppet Christmas Carol*, a Walt Disney Production.

Little Golden Books are books with which children grow. They are written to entertain, inform, and stretch the child's imagination. The stories and illustrations have made them favorites with children and parents for over 50 years. The stories are classics like *Snow White and the Seven Dwarfs* as well as new favorites. Cookie Monster is in *Cookie Monster and the Cookie Tree*.

Henson's Muppets are famous throughout the world. From 1975 to 1981 "The Muppet Show" television program was estimated to have attracted 235 million viewers in 100 countries. At the time of Jim Henson's death, the spring of 1990, another successful show was airing, "The Muppet Babies."

The Cookie Monster is made of recycled plastic. The plastic is blue and has a shaggy sculptured design. The details are painted on the 9" bottle. It was retailed in 1993. Information molded in the bottom of the bottle includes: "SOFT SOAP INT. INC./GAHASKA, MN 55318/BOTTLE MADE IN CHINA/®JHP INC." (Jim Henson Productions Inc.)

Batman Bubble Bath was marketed by "Kid Care.®" Printed on the label on the bottom of the 10", blue plastic bottle: "BATMAN, THE DARK KNIGHT and all related slogans and logos are trademarks of DC Comics Inc.® 1991." Copyright information is also molded into the bottle: "™ & ®1991 DC Comics Inc. TSUMURA INT'L. INC./MADE IN THAILAND."

Kid Care® also marketed The Little Mermaid Bubble Bath in 9" plastic bottles. It is a trademark character of the Walt Disney Company. Marks include "1991 TSUMURA INTERNATIONAL INC./®THE WALT DISNEY COMPANY/MADE IN THAILAND."

A very detailed "Kid Care" bottle is Snow White®, with the Walt Disney Company copyright. The 9½" bottle is filled with 10 ounces of bubble bath. Marks molded into base: "®1993 TSUMURA INT'L INC./©THE WALT DISNEY COMPANY/BOTTLE MADE IN THAILAND." (The bottle was filled in the U.S.A.)

Cookie Monster — 1993 Jim Henson Productions Inc.®, Soft Soap Int. Inc., 9", plastic, $10.00.

Batman — 1991 DC Comics Inc.®, Tsumura Int'l Inc., 10", plastic, $10.00.

Little Mermaid — 1991 Walt Disney Company®, Tsumura Int'l Inc., 9", plastic, $10.00.

Snow White — 1993 Walt Disney Product.®, Tsumura Int'l Inc., 9½", plastic, $10.00.

Belle®, of *Beauty and the Beast*, also has the Walt Disney Company copyright. The 8½" bottle, made basically of recycled plastic, was distributed by Cosrich Div. PMC Inc. in 1991.

"You ain't never had a friend like me!" Genie®, the wise cracking guy that changes from wispy images of smoke to the round, huggable Genie with a top knot, is the main attraction in the Walt Disney's *Aladdin*.

The tales of Aladdin and the Arabian Nights have intrigued people for hundreds of years, some say thousands. "Aladdin and His Wonderful Lamp" is a story in the book, *The Thousand and One Nights*, a collection of stories started long before books were made.

After the Walt Disney Studios took the public on a magic carpet ride from the ends of the earth to the Sultan's palace in Agrabah, the Magic Genie and Princess Jasmine® became promotional characters through licensing agreements with the Walt Disney Company. Two 1993 characters are plastic bottles filled with bubble bath. The heads of Genie and Jasmine are a softer vinyl that slips over the lid of the bottles. On the bottom of each bottle, molded into the plastic are the following marks: "®THE WALT DISNEY COMPANY/DIST BY COSRICH DIVISION, PMC INC/PERTH AMBOY, NJ 08861/BOTTLE MADE IN CHINA."

**Belle — 1991
Walt Disney Company®,
Cosrich Div. PMC Inc.,
8½", plastic, $10.00.**

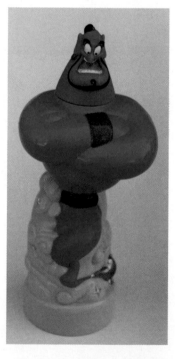

**Magic Genie — 1993
Walt Disney Company®,
Cosrich Div. PMC Inc.,
8½", plastic, $10.00.**

**Princess Jasmine — 1993
Walt Disney Company®,
Cosrich Div. PMC Inc.,
9", plastic, $10.00.**

Tootsietoy's Bubble Sets are a prime example of appealing to the fun side of every kid. When they are of the "bubble blowing age" what do they like? Who do they know? Every kid in America knows Donald Duck® and Minnie Mouse® from the Walt Disney cartoons. A bubble set with a bubble bottle in the image of a cartoon character is much more fun than a plain bottle. Just to be on the safe side, both types of bottles were included in the package!

Tootsietoy® retailed Minnie's Bubble Set® and the Sheriff Donald Duck Bubble Set® in the late 1980's. Each set includes the plastic bottle of "Wonder Bubbles®" (made in the U.S.A.) and a character bottle with a wand inside.

The Minnie Mouse toy is a two piece plastic bottle 5" tall. The head screws off and a wand is attached to the head. The Wonder Bubble® solution is then poured into the lower portion of the mouse body. Children are instructed to dip the wand carefully into the bubble solution and blow gently through the opening to create beautiful bubbles.

Marks on the bottom of the toy: "1986/The Walt Disney/Company/TOOTSIETOY® TOOTSIETOY is a division of Strombecker Corporation, Chicago, IL."

Sheriff Donald Duck is made somewhat differently. The hat screws off. The wand is attached to the hat. Wonder Bubble® is then poured into Donald's head. Marks on bottom of bottle: "The Walt Disney/Company/TOOTSIETOY®/MADE IN CHINA."

In the 1990's Barney, the lovable dinosaur was a favorite character. (See Chapter One.) The Barney Bubble Blower® was manufactured by Happiness Express Inc. New York, N.Y.

The contoured bottle in the image of Barney® is made of purple plastic and has painted features, a blue jacket and hat. It is filled with a wand and lots of bubbles, non-toxic but recommended for children three and over.

To use the wand and bubble blower, turn Barney's hat counterclockwise. Pull the hat wand out and blow the bubbles. This Barney is only 4½" tall. Marks molded in the bottom of the bottle, "1993 Lyons." Barney is a trademark of The Lyons Group.

**Donald Duck & Minnie Mouse — 1986
The Walt Disney Company, Tootsietoy®,
5", plastic, $5.00 each.**

**Barney — 1993
The Lyons Group®,
plastic, 4½", $5.00.**

CHRISTMAS ORNAMENTS

Christmas ornaments made in the image of company trademarks were prolific in the the 1980's and early 1990's. The Campbell Soup Company offered hand-painted, porcelain bisque Christmas ornaments in 1991 and 1992. The 1991 ornament is a 3" Campbell Kid® with a red Santa Claus suit and bag of toys. A miniature Campbell's Soup can with two Campbell Kids in it was offered in 1992. A Campbell Kid Soup Bowl, made of metal, was offered in 1993. Three kids are snuggled under a quilt in a Campbell bowl. The bowl is on a saucer decorated with miniature Christmas lights. Originally the decorations required two Campbell Soup labels and varied amounts of cash.

In November 1992, the Hershey Company offered two tree ornaments. They are handcrafted, wood characters with "Hershey" hats. One has a toboggan and the other a wagon loaded with a large chocolate Kiss®, a trademark of the Hershey Company. They required two proofs of purchase and $4.49 each.

Fancy Feast® Cat Food offered a hand crafted ornament featuring a big white cat in front of a fireplace and a Christmas tree in 1993. It was free with seven UPCs. The logo is included on the ornament.

**Campbell Kids — 1990's
Campbell Soup Company®, porcelain, $10.00.**

**Campbell Kids — 1993
Campbell Soup Company®, metal, $10.00.**

**Hershey Toboggan — 1992
Hershey Company®, 2½", wood, $10.00.**

**Fancy Feast Cat — 1993
Fancy Feast Cat Food® logo,
2½" x 3", hand crafted, $10.00.**

Sugar Bear™ — Kraft General Foods Inc.®.
Above: ©1993. Post® Golden Crisp® Cereal.
Left above: 1990, 3", cloth, $3.00.
Left: 1993, 2½", plastic, $5.00.

In 1990, a Sugar Bear trademark character was included in each box of Post® Golden Crisp® puffed wheat cereal. The free stuffed fabric bear has on a red Santa suit.

A plastic, 2½" Sugar Bear dressed like Santa Claus, with a red suit and green toy sack, was a 1993 promotion also included in boxes of cereal. Marks: "©1993 KRAFT GENERAL FOODS INC. MADE IN CHINA."

A Crayola Bear tree ornament was included in a Crayola® tin with 64 crayons in 1992. It is 3¼" tall and made of plastic. The drum is pine green and yellow.

Crayola Bear® — 1992
Binney & Smith Inc.®,
3¼", plastic, $5.00.

Trademark ornaments are also a "hot" retail item. Specialty shops carry an assortment of handcrafted Coca-Cola® Santas, produced under the authority of the Coca-Cola Company. The 1989 Coca-Cola Santa distributed by Willets is a favorite, inspired by illustrations and paintings of artists associated with Coca-Cola and available for reproduction only through the Coca-Cola Company. It is 3" tall. Good Old St. Nick is holding a bottle of Coca-Cola.

In 1993 the Coca-Cola Company introduced a new promotional character, a Coca-Cola Polar Bear®. It is 2¾" tall and made of plastic. The white bear is skating on a bottle cap and has a molded and painted red scarf around his neck. Both the scarf and the bottle cap have the Coca-Cola trademark.

Fast food restaurants offered several ornaments. Three different sets of "Waldo and Friends Holiday Ornaments®" were sold for 99 cents with a purchase at Hardee's® Food Systems Inc. in 1991. Set A included Snowman, Waldo with Woof and Waldo Watchers. Set B has Wizard White Beard, Waldo with books, and a Reindeer. Set C is Waldo with equipment, Woof and Wenda. The ornaments are 3–4" tall and are made of plastic. These are flat ornaments. They have a Martin Handford copyright and were manufactured in China.

McDonald's® had a miniature, 4½" doll in 1981. The cloth ornament has the features of the clown spokesman, Ronald®.

Far left: Santa Claus — 1989 Coca-Cola Company®, 3", handcrafted, $10.00.

Left: Polar Bear — 1993 Coca-Cola Company®, 2¾", plastic, $5.00.

Waldo & Friends — 1991 Martin Handford®, Hardee's Food Systems, 3"–4", plastic, $1.00 (each ornament).

Ronald — 1981 McDonald's Corp.®, 4½", cloth, $5.00.

The Swiss Miss® ornament is 3½" tall, made of white plastic. The features are painted. "SWISS MISS" is molded into the back of the flat ornament. Date is unknown.

Del Monte offered "Christmas Yumkins®" tree ornaments in 1991; a peach, pear, corn, pineapple, tomato, and pea. These plush trademark ornaments have tags sewn to each that reads: "©1991 DEL MONTE CORPORATION." They required five proofs-of-purchase and $2.20 for postage.

See Holiday Characters from Mars on page 97 for more tree ornaments and other holiday treasures.

**Swiss Miss —
Unknown date
Beatrice Foods
Company®,
3½", plastic,
$3.00.**

**Christmas Yumkins — 1991
Del Monte Corp.®, 4", plush, $2.00 (each ornament).**

FREE* YUMKIN ORNAMENTS
*WITH PURCHASE OF DEL MONTE PRODUCTS AND POSTAGE

DEL MONTE® YUMKIN™ ORNAMENTS MAIL-IN FORM
Offer valid through 2/28/93 or while supplies last.

For each set of six Yumkin Ornaments ordered, please send:
1. 5 proofs-of-purchase from any Del Monte products per set.
2. Check or money order for postage and handling, $2.20 per set.

Total # of sets ordered _____ x $2.20/set = _____ dollars
amt. enclosed

Total # of sets ordered _____ x 5 UPCs/set = _____ UPCs
enclosed

Number of children under 18 living at home? _____

MAIL TO: DEL MONTE YUMKIN ORNAMENTS, P.O. BOX 8744, CLINTON, IA 52736

Name _____

Address _____

City _____ State _____ Zip _____

Check or money order only, made payable to Del Monte Foods. Yumkin ornaments are 3" or 4" tall and meet all Federal safety standards for children's toys. Made especially for Del Monte. Not deliverable to P.O. Boxes. Good only in the U.S.A. Offer void where prohibited or restricted by state or local laws or regulations. Please allow 8-10 weeks for delivery. Manufacturer not responsible for late, lost or misdirected mail. NOT REDEEMABLE AT YOUR GROCERY STORE. OFFER VALID THROUGH 2/28/93 OR WHILE SUPPLIES LAST.
This order form may be copied.

Decorate for the holidays with a set of six Del Monte Yumkin™ ornaments.

Del Monte
Quality

©1992 Del Monte Foods, One Market Plaza, San Francisco, CA 94105

Del Monte® Yumkin™ ornaments. ©1992 Del Monte Foods.

CAMEL'S OLD JOE®

In December 1991 the R.J. Reynolds Tobacco Company, makers of Camel cigarettes, ran a full page ad on the inside cover of *Guns and Ammo* magazine. Old Joe has his Camel Cash in hand and a "Hard Pack Tour Jacket" is pictured. The ad says, "King of the Roadies, Only with Camel Cash. You don't have to eat road dust to get this slick Hard Pack Tour Jacket. Or a set of authentic Hard Pack Tumblers. Just use Camel Cash. It's good for lots of smooth stuff. So start savin' it up now. There's one C-note with all the details on every pack of filtered Camels. But ya gotta get it while the gettin's good. This tour ends May 31, 1992."

The "Hard Pack Collection" was available in the "Camel Cash Limited Edition Catalog!" The catalog also featured the "Smooth Collection," which includes Old Joe's can holder.

All this "smooth stuff" was restricted to smokers 21 years of age or older, and the orders had to be postmarked by May 31, 1992.

R.J. Reynolds, the tobacco division of RJR NABISCO Inc. was started in 1875 by R.J. Reynolds of Winston, North Carolina. Camel cigarettes were introduced in 1913. They are reported to have become the R.J. Reynolds Tobacco Companies best selling cigarette and they are sold in 135 countries.

Old Joe continues to encourage smokers to buy Camel Cigarettes in spite of concern about Old Joe influencing the underaged.

Camel's Old Joe — 1992
R.J. Reynolds Tobacco Company®, 4", vinyl, $15.00.

The J.I. Case Company, based in Racine, Wisconsin, was established in 1842. The company prospered and became the world's second largest agricultural equipment manufacturer, second to John Deere.

The first edition of the *J.I. Case Operator's Instruction Manual* for the "400" Series Tractors, 1955, lists modern farm machines made by Case: tractors, tractor implements, threshers, combines, plows, harrows, planters and listers, drills, cultivators, haying machinery like balers and rakes, beet and bean machinery and "other" machinery. The other machinery included corn pickers, forage harvesters, forage blowers, farm trucks and trailers, peanut plows, elevators, peanut liftrowers and hammer feed mills.

In 1967 the company was acquired by Tenneco Incorporated. International Harvester's agricultural equipment operations became a part of the business in 1985.

Through the years of expansion and success the bald eagle, standing on a globe, with "CASE" across the center, served as the J.I. Case emblem, a symbol of strength and power.

The eagle emblem was printed on the front cover of the manuals. Tin advertising signs included the emblem. Tractors and machines were marked with Case eagle emblems.

Early cast iron emblems, larger than life, adorned the entrances of J.I. Case dealerships.

Small cast iron counter displays were inside the establishments. They measure 8¼" with a round base. The Case eagle was the same on the front and back. "CASE" is molded across the globe. They are heavy and served as paperweights. Exact date unknown.

J.I Case Eagle — Date unknown J.I. Case Co.®, 8½", cast iron, $250.00.

CHARLIE TUNA®

Charlie the Tuna Squeeze Toy — 1973
Star-Kist Foods Inc.®, 7", vinyl, $35.00.

Charlie the Tuna Telephone — 1987
Star-Kist Foods Inc.®, 10", plastic, $50.00.

"Sorry Charlie. Star-Kist Tuna must be more than a tuna with good taste. It must be a tuna that tastes good."

Everyone knows Charlie, the bluefin tuna with an orange beret and pink sunglasses.

Since the day Star-Kist Foods Inc. decided to replace a Fisherman logo on the label of Star-Kist canned tuna with Charlie, he has tried to get *inside* the cans. It is Charlie's goal to be a Star-Kist product rather than the logo. Poor Charlie isn't good enough! For more than twenty years Charlie has faced rejection and ridicule but he never gives up. He continues to work and connive in television commercials and magazine ads as he tries to reach his goal.

Taken from a July 1972 *Good Housekeeping* magazine, a Charlie the Tuna bath scale premium advertisement reads: "For only $5.95 and 3 Star-Kist labels here's something that makes watching your weight almost fun. It's oval shaped and 13" x 10", covered with handsome white vinyl, and features Charlie in color. A fun and functional addition to any bathroom or bedroom. The scale is made by Counselor and is accurate on any type floor. It has a capacity of 300 lbs." Remember that bluefin tuna, found in Atlantic and Pacific Ocean waters, may weigh as much as 1,000 pounds!

Company premiums and licensing agreements keep Charlie the Tuna active in another capacity. The molded and painted squeeze toy Charlie is 7" tall. Marks: "©1973 Star-Kist Foods Inc." is found at the base in the back. "CHARLIE" is molded into the front of the hat.

The Charlie Tuna Telephone was offered in 1987 for $19.95 and one Star-Kist Tuna label. This telephone is the latest in electronics. It can be used in either touch tone or rotary dial pulse telephone systems. Charlie's red eyes blink as the number is dialed and they light up when a call is received. The bluefin tuna phone is 10" tall.

"Energizer" brand alkaline batteries were introduced in 1980 by the Eveready Battery Company Inc., a division of the Ralston Purina Company since 1986.

The Eveready Battery Company hired Chiat/Day/ Mojo, an advertising agency in Venice, California, to plan the promotional campaign for the new product. Consequently the Energizer Bunny was introduced in the fall of 1989. It became a company trademark.

The public was bombarded with store displays, the Energizer Bunny gliding across the television screen during prime time, full page advertising in magazines and free premiums.

In 1990 a replica of the trademark, a plush Energizer Bunny, with removable mallet, drum and shoes, was offered to consumers in exchange for proofs-of-purchase from packages of Energizer batteries. The offer for the 18" toy expired December 31, 1990.

Another successful promotion was Energizer Bunny Gear, free with UPCs. All the kids on the block had to have it. Hot pink was "totally cool" and the hot pink cap with an embroidered Ener-

gizer Bunny was a hit. A black T-shirt with the Energizer Bunny on the front, and and an acid washed denim jacket with the Energizer Bunny on the back were the favorites. Even the mothers were wearing them!

The Energizer Bunny flashlight is made of molded vinyl. It is only 4" tall. A light shines from the drum when the upper leg is pressed. In 1991 this was a new lighting product added to the Eveready Battery Company's broad array of flashlights and lanterns for household, personal, and out-of-home use.

The Energizer Bunny "keeps going...and going...and going."

Energizer Bunny Flashlight — 1991 Eveready Battery Company®, 4", vinyl, $10.00.

Energizer Bunny™ offer. ©1990 Eveready Battery Company Inc.

GEOFFREY®

Geoffrey — 1989
Toys 'Я' Us®, 8½", plastic, $20.00.

Who do you know that is orange and brown…and is always sticking his neck out at Toys 'Я' Us stores? Geoffrey the giraffe, of course, the symbol of New Jersey based Toys 'Я' Us chain store of toys and children's clothing.

Charles Lasarus named his retailing business Toys 'Я' Us in 1978. By 1989 there were 478 stores including stores in Singapore, Canada, Hong Kong, Malaysia, Germany, France, Taiwan, and the United States.

Geoffrey the giraffe is the company logo, trademark, spokes character. We see his image on store fronts, in advertising, and printed on some toys. In 1989 Geoffrey had taken on three dimensions, standing 8½" tall.

The vinyl and plastic statuette has molded and painted features: a red shirt, blue pants, white shoes and gloves. Geoffrey stands on a green base and has one arm behind him and one in front with his #1 finger pointing upward.

Geoffrey appears to be a statuette, with no practical purpose. Read the packaging and discover it is a flashlight.

Marks on this trademark treasure include "GEOFFREY™" painted on the shirt and "Made in Macau" molded into the bottom of the base.

HOLIDAY CHARACTERS FROM MARS INC.®

Mars Inc. continues to cater to collectors. Now there are more collectibles to look for, 3½" "M & M®" trademark characters, made of plastic, in all the colors of the candies — brown, green, red, orange, and yellow.

They are made in both the peanut shape (oval) and the plain (round) shape with flesh-beige arms and legs, and white shoes and gloves. Features are molded and painted. The mouth, eyes, and brows are black. A white "m" is painted on the body.

A 1.48 oz. box of "M & M" chocolate candies is included in the packaging. Look at the back of the character. Turn the back carefully in the direction of the arrow and when it is fully open, fill with M & M's. To close, turn the back as far as you can. To dispense candy, turn the back carefully in direction of the arrow until you hear a click. I have the dispensers out all year long…everyday is a holiday!

Other "M & M" characters in the colors and shapes of the original candies are the Christmas tree decorations marketed as part of the packaging. The plastic characters serve as the lids on tubes of candies.

The 1988 ornaments are M & M characters with a red Santa Claus cap. The arms are spread wide. In 1989 the characters are skating on an "ice" rink. The 1990 ornaments have red Santa Claus hats and carry snowballs. The characters stand on a white "snow" base. The 1991 characters are the same except they have red skis.

In 1992 the characters have a red and white candy cane and the 1993 M & M Santa ornaments have a sled. All have the Mars copyright and date on the bottom, molded in the plastic.

Mars did not forget St. Valentine's Day. The 1992 packages of M & M's included cupid-like characters with a quiver and bow. A "LOVE" red heart is also on the base.

In 1994, Easter "M & M" characters, hatching from eggs, have taken on the pastel colors of the new Holiday Chocolate Candies®…blue, lavender, pink, green, and yellow. The advertising theme is "Everyone likes to dress up for the holidays. So do we."

Olympic events aren't exactly a holiday but I am including the "M & M" Olympic characters of the 1990's in this section. They were included in the packaging as well. The Olympic characters are in the two shapes and all colors of the original M & M's. Each one has sports equipment — an Olympic torch, soccer balls, hurdles, skis, hockey sticks, ice skates, and weights. These characters represent Mars's support of the Olympic Games in 1992.

Two larger characters marketed by Mars Inc. are the Halloween containers, an orange plastic pumpkin with a "Milky Way®" sticker, and a "Snickers®" ghost. Both are 8" tall and the lid is removable. Molded on the bottoms of the characters, "®MARS INC. 1990."

M & M dispensers — 1991
Mars Inc.®, 3½", plastic, $10.00 each.

M & M's Christmas (hat & snowballs) — 1990
Mars Inc.®, 2½"–3",
plastic, $3.00 each.

M & M's Christmas — 1988 (hat) & 1989 (hat & skates)
Mars Inc.®, 2½"–3", plastic, $3.00 each.

M & M's Christmas (red ski) — 1991
Mars Inc.®, 3", plastic, $3.00 each.

M & M's Christmas (candy cane) — 1992
Mars Inc.®, 2½"–3", plastic, $3.00 each.

M & M's Valentines — 1992
Mars Inc.®, 2½"–3", plastic, $3.00 each.

M & M's Easter (Easter basket) — 1992
Mars Inc.®, 2½"–3", plastic, $3.00 each.

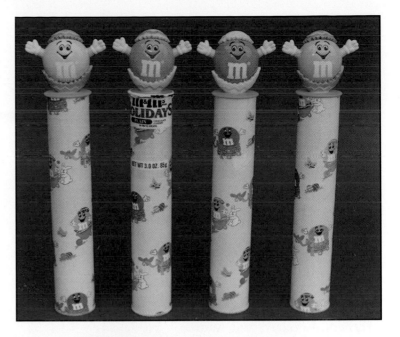

M & M's Easter (hatching) — 1994
Mars Inc.®, 2½"–3", plastic, $3.00 each.

M & M's Olympic — 1990
Mars Inc.®, 2½"–3", plastic, $3.00 each.

Milky Way Pumpkin & Snickers Ghost — 1990
Mars Inc.®, 8"–8½", plastic, $5.00 each.

MR. BIBENDUM®

The company slogan is "Michelin, because so much is riding on your tires."

The logo for the Michelin Tire Corporation is known by several names, the Michelin Tire Man, Mr. Bibendum, or simply and affectionately Old Bib by company employees.

Old Bib! How old is old? Mr. Bibendum originated in 1898 when the two Michelin brothers, Edouard and André, were visiting an exhibition in Lyon, France. They came across a display of tires stacked one on top of the other. Edouard Michelin's inventive imagination was aroused. He remarked to his brother that if the tires had arms, they would resemble a man.

Several months later André was working on an advertisement with an artist, O'Galop, when he was attracted to a poster picture of a large man raising a stein of beer. The caption said, "Nunc est bibendum," a latin phase meaning "Now is the time to drink."

Mr. Bibendum Display — 1981 Michelin Tire Company®, 12", plastic, $50.00.

Mr. Bibendum Key Chain — 1960's, 1½", $25.00.

One thing led to another and O'Galop was instructed to draw a man made of tires, holding a champagne glass full of tire hazards…glass, nails, and you name it. The caption, "Nunc est bibendum — To your health — The Michelin Tire Swallows Obstacles," was printed on the new advertisement.

The ad was an immediate success but Bibendum was not officially christened until Thery, the famous race driver, was preparing for the Paris-Amsterdam race and shouted as André passed, "I say, there goes Bibendum!" Bib's popularity spread throughout the world. It is one of the oldest and most recognized trademarks, symbolizing Michelin service to the driving public in over 150 countries.

Mr. Bibendum is widely recognized by young and old alike as a Michelin spokesman. The congenial Michelin man is a symbol of Michelin's pioneering leadership and high standard of technological achievement.

The original Mr. Bibendum was composed of shapes representing the tires of the late 1800's, narrow straight-edged tires. There was also a cigar and pince-nez glasses. Eventually the tires became more round and much wider. The cigar and glasses were removed.

Mr. Bibendum was never a static figure. Consumers see him in many positions, walking, jumping, running and even flying, as he promotes Michelin tires. He is found in sizes from the 50-foot inflatable character to key-chain ornaments.

Michelin Tire dealers decorate their pickup trucks with child size, white vinyl Michelin Men bolted to the truck box or on the cab. They have baseball caps on their heads and "MICHELIN" is clearly painted across their chests for all to see.

A white plastic Mr. Bib, 12" tall was made in 1981, a desk top version of the Michelin trademark. Marks: "MICHELIN" on the banner across the chest. (Courtesy of the Michelin Tire Company.)

"Mr. Bubble®, America's favorite Bubble Bath for kids. The bubble bath that makes getting clean almost as much fun as getting dirty!"

In the 1970's Mr. Bubble bubble bath was sold in plastic containers that looked somewhat like pink snowmen. A round head was on top of a rather elongated body, balanced out with subtle feet. This was the Gold Seal Company Mr. Bubble.

In an ad in *Woman's Day*, July 29th, 1986, three different packages with Mr. Bubble, as we know him today, were featured with a 1984 DC Comics Inc. copyright. This leads me to believe the personified bubble, with the big round nose and eyes, was designed by someone in that company in 1984.

Mr. Bubble, the pink vinyl character, standing 8" tall, was available in 1990. Other Mr. Bubble premiums included a soft 10" Mr. Bubble doll, a Mr. Bubble rubber stamp, a Bath Time Puppet, Mr. Bubble bath and beach towels.

Collectors and kids could also have a "Bathtime cassette tape," to sing your "bubbles" away with Joanie Bartel's Magic Series of bathtime hits such as "Bubble Bath" and "Splish Splash."

Mr. Bubble Tub Pal was offered on Mr. Bubble bubble bath. The original cost was $8.45 and coupon.

The "Tub Pal" offered by Airwick Industries has the mark "Mr. Bubble®" incised on back of the body.

Mr. Bubble Tub Pal — 1990
Airwick Industries Inc.®, 8", vinyl, $35.00.

OLD CROW®

"Old Crow, the greatest name in bourbon" was first made by James Crow in 1835.

Trademark origin is often a mystery but obviously it did not require a scientific survey to come up with the idea to use the crow as a trademark for James Crow's product.

In an Old Crow advertisement in a 1947 *Life* magazine, there was pictured a large black crow, head down, appearing to be in his typical garden position, ready to scratch out the sweet corn seed!

My first thought was, this is hardly a trademark that would encourage consumers to buy the best...it would more than likely cause them to shout and wave their arms at a common pest! Others, no doubt, shared this view and perhaps lost a little sleep dreaming up a more appropriate symbol.

Three years later advertising featured the crow with a complete make over...standing tall in his hat and vest, a small symbol in the corner of a full page ad, in a 1950 *Life* magazine!

The history of the three dimensional trademark character evolves in *Life*. In a July 1964 issue of *Life*, the Old Crow logo has taken a new form. The crow is now a black plastic figurine in white shirt and red vest, black hat and bow tie. In fact in this particular ad there are six crows in a row and at the top of the page it says, "Don't just watch the birds..." After an interval of welcoming space the ad continues with "go buy..." and a picture of Old Crow Kentucky straight bourbon whiskey. Another paragraph encourages the consumer to "buy this birdie."

Several plastic Old Crow counter display figures of the 1950's and 60's are in existence. The 13½" character stands on a round base. A 10" figure is the same as the one used in the *Life* ads. The third Old Crow is only 5½" tall.

The three counter displays are well marked, inscribed or painted in the front of the base, "OLD CROW." On the back of the figures "KENTUCKY STRAIGHT BOURBON WHISKEY 86 PROOF/DISTILLED AND BOTTLED BY THE FAMOUS OLD CROW DISTILLERY CO./FRANKFORT KY," or "KENTUCKY WHISKEY" and "OLD CROW DISTILLERY CO./FRANKFORT KY."

Old Crow — Old Crow Distillery Company®
Plastic, from left to right: 1956, 13½", $75.00;
1960's, 10", $50.00; & 1960's, 5½", $25.00.

Old Crow Distillery Co., *Life* 1964.

PEZ HEADS®

Pez Heads, Pezzie Party, Pez Conventions, Piggy on a Purple Stick, Santa Claus — with feet; the Pez-a-holic lingo is sweeping the country from coast to coast.

How do Pez Heads qualify as zany characters of the ad world? Some are definitely advertising or trademark characters such as Peter Pez, the Pez clown logo. This clown is used in store displays and he is recognized by the bright yellow hair and blue hat with "PEZ" painted on it.

Pez Candy Inc. use other licensed trademark characters such as the Spider-Man trademark of the Marvel Comics Group, Batman from DC Comics Inc., Jim Henson's Muppets, Bugs Bunny from Warner Bros. Inc,

and the Peanuts Gang from United Features Syndicate. There are hundreds, for collectors of all ages, to find.

Santa Claus is one of the most popular characters used in advertising. Pez Candy Inc. has sold several different kinds, with feet, without feet, full bodied or the head only.

Pez candies were first made by Edouard Haas of Austria in 1927. It wasn't until the 1940's that the Pez dispensers were invented.

Austria, Yugoslavia, Hong Kong, and the United States all have claim to the dispensers. Each Pez stem has molded markings indicating the country of origin. Pez candy is made in Orange, Connecticut.

Pez Heads — Dates unknown
Pez Inc.®, 4"–5", plastic, $1.29–$25.00 each.

Right:
Peter Pez, Pez Inc.®,
Spider-Man, Marvel Comics Group®.
Batman, DC Comics Inc.®

Below left:
Santa Claus, Pez Inc.®,
Miss Piggy, Jim Henson Muppets®.
Bugs Bunny, Warner Bros.®

Below right:
The Peanuts Gang: Charlie Brown, Snoopy, and Lucy.
United Features Syndicate®.

A.A. Milne did what any good father would do. He gave his son, Christopher Robin Milne, a teddy bear for his first birthday. The bear was about the color of butterscotch candy, soft and plush to hold and love. They named it Winnie-the-Pooh in 1921.

A.A. Milne told his son stories and he used Christopher Robin as a character in the stories. Winnie-the-Pooh was his teddy bear in the stories too. The teddy bear was called Pooh or Pooh Bear or Winnie-the-Pooh. He was definitely a "bear of little brain," but Pooh was a good bear and he had friends.

Eeyore the donkey was one friend, often sad and on the side lines. There was also Piglet, small but willing to help, and the bouncy boisterous Tigger the Tiger!

A.A. Milne no doubt witnessed a child's excitement and intrigue with Pooh stories and compiled a book about Christopher and Pooh. *When We Were Very Young*, by A.A. Milne was published in 1924 and over a half million copies sold.

The history between 1924 and 1960 is sketchy but sometime in the 60's Winnie-the-Pooh took on new dimensions. The Walt Disney Company acquired exclusive rights to A.A. Milne's Winnie-the-Pooh and cartoons and features were made and shown all over the world.

Toy companies produced more Pooh Bears. Winnie-the-Pooh was in the Little Golden Books. Winnie-the-Pooh became famous! and is still going strong!

In 1991 Johnson & Johnson offered Johnson's Bath Buddies: Tigger's Bath Bubbles®, Eeyore's Conditioning Detangler®, Pooh's No more Tears Shampoo®, and Piglet's Liquid Bath® that "makes bath time a laugh time!"

The products are marketed in white plastic containers with paper wrappers that can easily be removed. The decorative lids, Pooh and his friends, were made in China. Each product and character carries two trademarks: "®J&J CPI 1991" and the "WALT DISNEY COMPANY."

Pooh and Friends — 1991
Walt Disney Company®, J & J CPI 1991®, 8", plastic, $5.00 each.

QUAKER OATS®

The Aunt Jemima Mills Company dates back to 1903 and it became a part of the Quaker Oats Company in 1926. The company chose a cheerful image of a black cook, by the name of Aunt Jemima, to represent the Aunt Jemima Pancake Flour. Consumers became familiar with her in advertising and on product labels.

In a 1916 ad in *Ladies' Home Journal*, Aunt Jemima is pictured with a striped dress, polka-dot shawl, a turban and a white apron. At this time Nancy Green was the model for Aunt Jemima. The words, "I'se in town Honey," accompanied the ads.

There was a special rag doll offer with the ad. For 10¢ in stamps or coins and three tops from the packages of either Aunt Jemima Pancake Flour or Buckwheat Flour the consumer could have the Aunt Jemima Rag Doll Family, a set of four dolls.

Two years later there was a new ad: "Send one Aunt Jemima box top (either Pancake or Buckwheat Flour) with only six cents in stamps and get one of the famous Aunt Jemima Rag Dolls. Or send four tops and only twenty-four cents for Aunt Jemima and Uncle Mose, and two cunning pickaninnies [an unacceptable word in America today], all in bright colors ready to cut and stuff. Send to Aunt Jemima Mills Company, St. Joseph, Missouri."

Aunt Jemima and Uncle Mose have appeared as spice sets, cookie jars, syrup pitchers, wall pieces, salt and pepper shakers. The most popular are the items made by the F & F Mold & Die Works in the 1950's.

Salt and pepper shakers in the likeness of the early Aunt Jemima and Uncle Mose were reproduced in the 1980's. They are 3½" tall (same as the 1950's set) and made of red molded plastic. Although they are very similar, markings on the bottom prevent anyone from making a mistake that they are old. Embossed on the bottom of both characters: "Miss Martha/Originals Inc./Antique Repro."

Quaker Oats used the Quaker Man for their logo and in the 1950's the company offered a 3½" plastic pitcher in the image of the Quaker Man.

Ken-L-Ration pet food was another Quaker product and in the 1950's. Fi-Fi and Fido were logos for the pet food and trademarks of Quaker Oats. Plastic salt and pepper shakers were made in the image of the dog and cat. "F & F MOLD & DIE WORKS" is molded on the bottom of each.

Quaker Oats Characters

Fi-Fi & Fido — 1950's, Ken-L-Ration pet food trademark, F&F Mold & Die Works, 3", plastic, $20.00; Quaker Man pitcher — 1950's, Quaker Oats Oatmeal®, 3½", plastic, $25.00; Aunt Jemima & Uncle Mose — 1980's, Miss Martha Originals Inc. Antique Reproductions, 3½", plastic, $10.00.

Aunt Jemima and Uncle Mose — 1950's. All are courtesy of Leora Sullivan.

Left to right: 5½" syrup pitcher, "AUNT JEMIMA" molded on back, "F&F/Mold & Die Works/Dayton, Ohio/Made in U.S.A.," on bottom, red plastic, $65.00; 3½" salt and pepper, names molded on each, F&F Mold & Die Works identification on bottoms, red plastic, $35.00; 5⅛" salt and pepper, same marks as smaller set. $50.00.

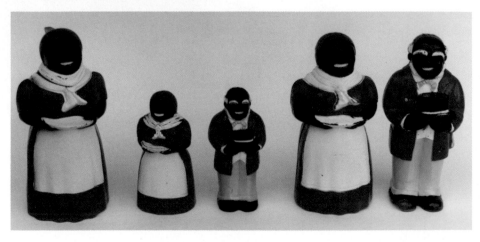

"You make me laugh, I like the Sprite in you!" Press the button under the can of Sprite in Lucky Lymon's hand and it will speak to you.

The Coca-Cola Company introduced Sprite in 1961. In one report, Sprite is mentioned as the world's #1 lemon-lime soft drink on the market.

Other soft drinks sold by the Coca-Cola Company are Diet Sprite®, Coca-Cola Classic®, Diet Coke®, Caffeine-Free Coca-Cola®, Caffeine-Free Diet Coke®, Cherry Coke®, Diet Cherry Coke®, Minute Maid®, Diet Minute Maid®, Fresca®, Hi-C®, Mello Yello®, Mr. Pibb®, Ramblin Root Beer®, and more!

The soft drink products are sold in over 160 countries. The Coca-Cola Company is the world's largest soft drink producer and one of the United States leading producers of citrus products.

Lucky Lymon, a vinyl lemon-lime character, appears in the 1990's as cheerful as morning sunshine, promoting with the almost real voice. The character is 7" tall. The body is the shape of a lemon. The top half has molded eyes and mouth. The bottom half is painted green. The legs are made of green vinyl and have yellow painted stripes. The arms are yellow vinyl and have green painted stripes. The markings are on the miniature can of Sprite: "SPRITE® GREAT LYMON® TASTE." Molded in back of body: "LUCKY LYMON®/MADE IN CHINA."

Sprite's Lucky Lymon (talks) — 1990's
Coca-Cola Company®, Sprite®, 7", vinyl, $25.00.

WILLIE & MILLIE

Willie retired in the early 60's. He worked for the Brown & Williamson Tobacco Corporation, a subsidiary of B.A.T. Industries in London, England.

Brown & Williamson Tobacco Corporation headquarters are in Louisville, Kentucky, with manufacturing in Macon, Georgia; Winston-Salem, North Carolina; and Lancaster, Pennsylvania.

The company is spread out with leaf processing in Wilson, South Carolina, and leaf storage in Blacksburg, South Carolina.

What does all this have to do with Willie and Millie? According to consumer specialist Gayle Graham, the Brown & Williamson Tobacco Corporation introduced KOOL cigarettes in 1933. A penguin was featured as KOOL's advertising symbol to create the aura of coolness. As the popularity and recognition of the penguin grew, the name "Willie" was added in the late 1930's. The credit for designing Willie was given to the advertising agency which had the Kool brand cigarettes account.

Willie was busy. He appeared in magazines and billboards. His likeness was used on a variety of specialty advertising items. Collectors find him on key chains, cigarette lighters, and jewelry. The salt and pepper shakers are more than likely the most popular KOOL's collectible.

So the legend goes, while modeling for the salt and pepper shakers Willie met his wife, Millie. Together they represented the company that made the slogan, "For a treat instead of a treatment, smoke KOOL cigarettes," popular.

Willie and Millie salt and pepper characters are made of black, hard plastic and stand 3½" tall. They have molded and painted features. Their names are molded on the chest and "F & F MOLD & DIE WORKS, DAYTON, OHIO, USA," is on the bottom.

Willie is a "plain" penguin but Millie is something else. Look for a "Kool" character with dreamy eyes and painted lashes. She is definitely ready for a party with a red bow on her head and matching beads around her neck.

Willie & Millie — 1950
Brown & Williamson Tobacco Corp., F & F Mold & Die Works, 3½", plastic, $20.00.

CHAPTER FOUR

Advertising Dolls

A & W'S® GREAT ROOT BEAR®

The A & W Root Beer restaurants celebrated 75 years of business in 1994. Roy Allen and Frank Wright of Lodi, California, opened the first walk-in A & W restaurant in 1919, offering a limited menu of hot dogs and root beer. Root beer was five cents a mug.

A & W restaurants are now in 11 countries and 40 states in the U.S., with a total of 700 locations.

Although a bit more expensive, A & W root beer is the same today as it was in the beginning, a formula using a blend of healthful roots, barks, and herbs. The secret recipe includes wintergreen leaves, wild cherry bark, sarsaparilla root, althea root, spikenard, anise seed, angelica root, and birch bark. There are sixteen ingredients counting all spices and berries.

Although the beverage remains the same, the restaurants have changed. At first the A & W Root Beer walk-in restaurants were designed like a wooden root beer barrel with windows and doors. By 1950 the walk-ins were changed to drive-ins and young people dressed in orange and brown uniforms were the car hops, cheerfully serving customers in "Hot Rod Fords" and Chevys.

A & W kept some traditions. One favorite tradition is the serving of a free 3½ ounce mug of root beer to children under five. (There is no caffeine in A & W Root Beer). The orange and brown colors in advertising remain constant. The Great Root Bear is another tradition.

Store owners often own a Great Root Bear costume and the children's favorite bear comes to visit on special days. In 1975 a plush bear was sold over the counter, resembling the trademark bear. The 13" brown bear has an orange hat and shirt. The shirt is part of the body and it is not removable. The eyes are plastic. The mouth and nose are made of felt glued to the face. It was made in Korea.

Another Great Root Bear was available in 1994. This time the bear is made of plastic and stands 9" tall. It's actually a sipper with a plastic straw fitted into the top of the hat. The "A & W" patch is molded into the shirt. Other markings on the bottom, "®1994 A & W RESTAURANTS INC./CONTOUR BOTTLES 416-784-9399/MADE IN CANADA/DISHWASHER SAFE."

A & W Great Root Beer — A & W Restaurants Inc.®
Plush bear, 1975, 13", $15.00.
Plastic sipper, 1994, 9", $3.00.

BLACK FOREST GUMMY BEAR®

"The candies that don't stick to your teeth and if you eat one you can't stop!"

The Foreign Candy Company is a comparatively "new" company, in Hull, Iowa, incorporated in 1982 and owned privately by Peter and Betty De Yager. They said it all began in 1978 when Betty had resigned her position at Western Christian High School to stay at home and have their first child and they were looking for a home-based source of extra income. At that time Peter taught German language at Western Christian High.

It was from Peter's 1976 and 1977 summer experiences that they came up with the idea of starting a "foreign candy" company. Peter had taken groups of German students to Europe those two summers. One of the things the students enjoyed most in Europe was the delicious candy. Some of the favorite candies were the Toblerone chocolate bars (chocolate bars with almond and honey nougat) and the "Gummi Baerchen," (Gummi or Gummy Bears).

Upon returning home from the trip in 1977, the students were given an assignment to write a letter to the German Gummy Bear factory they had visited. In return the company surprised them by sending 10 cases of Gummy Bears to the school.

This was when Peter had the idea of selling Gummy Bears to German clubs/teachers across the U.S. Soon their house, garage, and two neighbor's garages were full of candy! In 1980, Peter made the decision to resign his teaching job. He and his father bought some land in Hull and built their first building for the growing business.

In 1989, Gummy Dinosaurs, Gummy Hearts, Gummy Christmas Trees, Gummy Rabbits, and Gummy Halloween Treats were added. They were always coming up with new ideas. In 1992 "Gummy Chevys" were introduced.

The Foreign Candy Company Incorporated used the 19", plush Gummy Bear as a short term incentive premium to dealers. It was free with each prepack order. (The Black Forest Gummy Bear is compliments of The Foreign Candy Company Incorporated.)

Black Forest Gummy Bear — 1992
The Foreign Candy Company, 19", plush, $35.00.

BURGER KING®

In 1988 British Grand Metropolitan bought Pillsbury and acquired Burger King in the deal.

Burger King restaurants are distinguished by the slogan, "Have it your way at Burger King." Their Burger King character dolls were first offered in 1972 and 1973. Both dolls are 16" tall, have out-flung arms, short legs, a gold crown, a yellow suit and red robe. The only noticeable difference in the two is the markings. The 1972 is unmarked where the 1973 doll wears a medallion with "BURGER KING" printed on it. "BURGER KING" and the date is also printed on the back of each foot. The cloth pre-stuffed dolls were made by Chase Bag Company and they sold for $1.00 over the Burger King counters.

The third doll, offered in 1977, is a slim Burger King resembling the TV Burger King on the company commercial. This trademark doll measures 15". There were other changes too. Cartoon type features were changed to realistic eyes and a red beard and mustache on a round face. Two markings are visible. A medallion at the neck and the belt buckle have "BURGER KING" printed on them. This cloth doll was also made by the Chase Bag company. The new streamlined Burger King was advertised as a "free" doll. In this promotion the consumer was required to purchase a booklet of coupons at a cost of $5.00 to receive the "free" doll. Another Burger King doll was made in 1980 by the Knickerbocker Toy Company. It is a real treasure.

The doll measures 20", has a velour body, vinyl head and hands, molded red hair, and a curled mustache. Its suit is red velour and is not removable. He wears yellow plastic boots. The gold molded crown is a part of the head, and "©1980 Burger King Corp." is molded on the back of the crown. A cloth tag on the body says, "The Magical BURGER KING, MANUFACTURED UNDER LICENSE FROM BURGER KING CORPORATION, MIAMI, FLORIDA, U.S.A. BY KNICKERBOCKER TOY COMPANY, MIDDLESEX, N.J."

By 1990 the burger corporation was following the trend of licensing trademark characters belonging to other companies.

The Simpsons™ were stars in 1990. Dolls were offered on a Burger King TV commercial. They were exclusive Burger King Simpson dolls, available for five weeks. Each week a new doll was offered. They were $3.49 each and a purchase of either blueberry muffins or fries.

Like other promotions, this one was fast and furious, and many collectors were leaving empty handed if they did not go to Burger King early in the week. It appeared as if every collector and kid on the block had to have a doll, and if they could have but one, it was Bart Simpson!

They are not difficult to spot. Their egg yolk yellow heads and golf ball eyes stand out and they all have tags sewn to the body, "The Simpsons™/MATT GROENING ©1990 20TH C FOX F.C."

The dolls have vinyl heads and cloth bodies. The father figure, Homer, is 11" tall and wears a white shirt and light blue pants. Marge (Mom) is 13" tall, which includes 3" of bright blue molded hair. She exhibits a passion for brilliant colors, with red shoes and necklace and green dress. Bart, from the tip of his spike hair cut to his toes, measures 9", and his original clothes are a peach T-shirt and blue pants. Sister Lisa is 8" tall and draws attention in a red dress. Baby Maggie is 7" tall, and wears a blue sleeper. She also has a red pacifier in her mouth.

Burger King® – 1973
Burger King Corp., 16", cloth, $10.00.

Burger King® — 1977
Burger King Corp., 15", cloth, $10.00.

Burger King® — 1980
Burger King Corp., Knickerbocker Toy Co.,
20", cloth & vinyl, $20.00.

The Simpson Family — 1990
™Matt Groening, ©20th Century Fox F.C.,
Burger King Corp., 7"–13", cloth and vinyl, set of five $50.00.

CAMPBELL SOUP KIDS®

Campbell Kids — 1950
Campbell Soup Co.®, salt and pepper, plastic, $35.00.
Campbell Soup Co.® cup, plastic, $12.00.

Campbell Kid — 1964
Campbell Soup Co.®, 10", vinyl, $25.00.

Below: Bicentennial Campbell Kids — 1976
Campbell Soup Co.®, 10", vinyl, $35.00 each.

The Campbell Kids (with no first names) never grow old. Artist Grace Gebbie Drayton created the Campbell Kids in 1904. Through the years other artists and studios have worked on the Campbell Kids trademark, making minor changes, designing dolls, and using the trademark characters in commercials and advertising.

It was not until 1956 that the Campbell Soup Company offered the Campbell Kid dolls as premiums and the tradition continues.

Campbell Kids offered in 1964 are 10" vinyl dolls, jointed at neck, hip, and shoulders. The hair is molded and painted. One doll was available for $2.00 and two product labels. There were several different costumes for the dolls.

Perhaps the most popular Campbell Kids were the Bicentennial Kids in colonial costumes. They are actually the same doll as the 1964 dolls.

The February 1976 *Ladies' Home Journal* featured the ad, "Here are the Campbell Kids the way they would have looked 200 years ago!" The color ad pictured the pair with a bowl of Campbell's Soup in front of them. Each doll required $4.95 and four labels from any Campbell's Vegetable Soup. The expiration date was December 31, 1976.

The "Special Edition Kid Dolls" were offered in 1988. Dolls are vinyl, jointed at neck, shoulder, and hip and marked on the back of the head, "Campbell's Soup Company."

These dolls have rooted synthetic hair and were manufactured by House of Globe Art. The original cost was $8.99 and two Campbell Soup labels.

The Campbell Kids of America Series was available to collectors until May 31, 1994. These special dolls were offered at a special price in celebration of the 125th Anniversary of the Campbell Soup Company and the 90th birthday of the Campbell Kids. Designed by Francine Cee Collectibles, they are sculptured in "fine collector's vinyl" and stand 16" tall. The hand painted head and softly blushed five-piece jointed body allows you to change their pose anytime. They have synthetic hair. There is a pair of each, the Traditional, Native American, and African American, priced for $125.00.

Other items in the image of the Campbell Kids are the the set of salt and pepper shakers made in the 50's. "PERMISSION OF THE CAMPBELL SOUP COMPANY" is incised in the plastic.

Campbell Kid cups, made of plastic, are also popular items. The date is unknown.

There's romance and history in Campbell's Tomato Soup—

Campbell Soup Co., *Ladies' Home Journal*, August 1916.

Special Edition Kid Dolls — 1988
Campbell Soup Co.®,
10", vinyl, $25.00 each.

Campbell Kids™ of America Series — 1994
Campbell Soup Co.®, Francine Cee Collectibles, 16", vinyl, $125.00.

CAMPBELL'S VLASIC STORK®

Every time I purchased a jar of Vlasic Pickles®, and saw the stork with eye glasses, printed on the lid, I questioned, what is the connection between pickles and the stork? Why did Vlasic Foods choose a stork as the spokesbird in advertising?

According to the information sent to me by Associate Marketing Manager Sheila Bravo, this is the story:

"In order to create a unique personality for Vlasic Pickles that would differentiate them from competitive pickles, the first television campaign (1967) was based on the folklore that pregnant women crave pickles...and the only pickles they crave are Vlasic Pickles. After all, who is more of a pickle expert than a pregnant woman? This made the product unique because only a Vlasic Pickle gets pampered more than a pregnant woman.

In 1970, the campaign was broadened to 'Vlasic...the pampered pickle for pampered people.'

Four years later the company decided to return to the pregnancy theme. The Vlasic Stork was created by W.B. Doner, an advertising agency in Southfield, Michigan.

In 1974, the stork, a bird long associated with pregnancy and childbirth, was added to the advertising. He was introduced with the theme, "With the birth rate down and Vlasic Pickles sales up, I deliver Vlasic Pickles now."

There are other interesting facts in the Vlasic Pickle story. In the beginning Vlasic Foods was a milk delivery business owned by Joseph Vlasic in 1919, however it wasn't until 1945 that Joseph began distributing pickles under the Vlasic name. In 1959 Vlasic Foods began concentrating on the pickle packing business.

Almost 20 years later, in 1978, Vlasic Foods merged with the Campbell Soup Company.

We know the reputation of the Campbell Soup Company for offering premium dolls, cups, Christmas decorations and other trademark treasures. The Vlasic Stork was also offered as a premium.

In 1990 a full page ad in the Sunday advertising supplements featured a beautiful plush stork, 23" tall. This white bird has a red bow tie and a blue and white hat with "Vlasic" printed on it. The offer expired September 30, 1990. It was $17.95 plus two proofs-of-purchase.

Vlasic Stork — 1990
Campbell Soup Co.®, 23", plush, $20.00.

The wonderful Wizard of Os...that is SpaghettiOs®! This trademark of Campbell's Soup Company was available in exchange for $1.00 and two labels from either Franco-American SpaghettiOs or Ravioli in 1978 and 1979.

The Franco-American Food Company was acquired by the Campbell Soup Company in 1915.

These canned products are fast and easy foods with wholesome tomatoes, enriched pasta, and real cheese. Some have miniature meatballs made of beef.

The Wizard of Os logo has retired and we see the personified Os on the labels, the character with tennis shoes and stick legs, always on either a skateboard, a bike, or rollerblades. The slogan of 1993 was "I'm the O on the go and I go for SpaghettiOs!"

Look for a character with white hair covered with a wide brimmed, tall pointed hat, the color of SpaghettiO sauce. Six tiny Os decorate the hat. They are a pale yellow, not quite the same color as pasta...but we get the idea. The eyes are set closely together and rest on a wide nose. Molded eyelids give the Wizard a sleepy look.

The 8" vinyl doll has molded and painted clothes. The head moves. Identification on the bottom of the doll are the following marks: "WIZARD OF Os™ CAMPBELL SOUP COMPANY."

Wizard of Os — 1978
Campbell's Soup Co.®, 8", vinyl, $20.00.

COCA-COLA® SANTA CLAUS & BEAR

Coca-Cola Rushton Santa — 1957
Coca-Cola Co.®, 15", plush and vinyl,
glass bottle, $100.00.

Coca-Cola Polar Bear — 1993
Coca-Cola Co.®, Amoco Oil Co., 6½", plush, $5.00.

Have you noticed, about the time retailers are changing colors from orange and black to red and green, Santa Claus is advertising for the Coca-Cola Company?

Coca-Cola started this advertising tradition in 1931. They hired an artist, Haddon Sundblom, to create a realistic version of Santa Claus to use on all types of Christmas advertising, from billboards to magazine ads.

Along with Santa Claus there is always a slogan like, "Things go better with Coke®," and, "For real refreshment ...always pause for a Coke!" or, "Be really refreshed...Love that Coke!"

The first promotional Coca-Cola Santa Claus dolls were designed by Mrs. Mary Phillips Rushton, based on the character created by Sundblom for advertising. The Rushton Company of Atlanta, Georgia, manufactured the dolls in 1957. Thousands of dolls were distributed as premiums with company coupon offers.

Santa is 15" tall. The body, legs, and arms are red plush fabric stuffed with polyfoam. A white fur-like trim is on the wrists and legs. A hat is also red, trimmed with white. Boots may be either black or white. Neither the suit nor hat are removable. Santa's face, hands and boots are made of vinyl and the belt a lightweight black plastic. He holds a miniature bottle of Coke in his right hand, an important detail that is often missing.

During the Christmas season of 1993, there was a new turn of events in Coca-Cola advertising. Santa was replaced in the commercials with a white polar bear! The theme for the day..."Taste it all!"

Consequently the Coca-Cola trademark Polar Bear was used as a premium. A free Coca-Cola Polar Bear was offered by the Amoco Oil Company to customers. The first 12,000 eligible requests were honored. After the 12,000 Polar Bears were given out, people were given a gift certificate good for a free 2-liter bottle of Coca-Cola product at participating Amoco locations.

The same polar bear, with the "Always Coca-Cola" button on his chest, was offered at a discount to draw customers to Hardee's restaurants during the Christmas season in 1993.

A tag sewn to the toy has, "Coca-Cola® Brand Plush Design/®1993 The Coca-Cola Company/All Rights Reserved" printed on it. A paper tag in the bear's ear pictures the TV Coca-Cola Polar Bear and has the following words inside: "The Bear Everyone Is Thirsting After! You've seen him on TV delighting fans in millions of dens across the country. This is the one and only Coca-Cola Bear. A lovable visitor from the frozen North, he's guaranteed to warm the home of any family he joins."

"...and a Merry Christmas to all"

©1956 The Coca-Cola Company. *National Geographic*, 1956.

COCO WHEAT® CLAN

Coco Wheat Clan — Little Crow Foods®
12", plush, $15.00 each.
1991, CoCo Bunny; 1988, CoCo Bear; & 1990, CoCo Kitty.

Have you ever gone to the "supermarket jungle" with a well organized grocery list but in spite of the best of intentions you take home purchases you really hadn't planned on?

Picture this, if you will. A consumer who appears to be organized stops for a free sample of shrimp and sauce...and with the tiny napkin provided, she blots her mouth...smiles, and says "Thank You." She did not buy!

According to Vance Packard in *The Hidden Persuaders*, 80 percent of the housewives would have bought the product, and the women's husbands and children are more prone to splurge than that!

This experienced consumer was well aware of these facts and she continued shopping, proud of herself for not buying on impulse.

All was going well until the last aisle and the last item on the shopping list, Quaker's Quick Oatmeal®. It was on the bottom shelf and Mrs. Market Master bent down and picked up the 4½ pound package. As she straightened she seemed to be hypnotized by a box located on a shelf at eye level.

The box was an attractive red and yellow package of CoCo Wheats with a cocoa-colored baby bear on the front. Then the consumer broke the first rule in prevention of impulse buying. She picked up the package for closer inspection! The consumer turned the package over and found a little girl with a bubbling smile and wearing a red night gown. The girl in the ad was cheek to cheek with CoCo Bear and Little Crow Foods was offering the most irresistible baby bear this side of the Rocky Mountains to anyone that sent in $11.75 and one UPC!

If you're a collector of advertising dolls and characters you know what happened next!

The plush cocoa-colored 12" Bear was a premium in 1988. In July of 1990 the CoCo Kitty was offered on the CoCo Wheats package. It was 12" high, made of cream, fur-like fabric. Another member of the CoCo Wheat Clan was offered in July of 1991 during the "Snuggle up with CoCo Bunny" promotion.

Crayola Bear — 1986
Crayola®, ©Graphics International Inc., 6", plush, $5.00 each.

"Crayola. Childhood isn't childhood without it." Since 1903, children have enjoyed Crayola crayons. They start when they are about three with a box of basic colors and learn the difference between red, yellow, and blue.

By the time the children go to school the primary colors are "boring" and parents are pressured into buying the latest Crayola crayons with yellow-green, red-violet, and blue-green. Mom also gets a color book and sits down with Junior and colors one page while Junior sits beside her and colors the other page.

"Mom...I need silver for the wheels on this car. Mom...you should have a copper color for your tea kettle! Mom...if I had gold I would make this star gold!" Mom makes a mental note. Get Junior a new box of Crayola crayons for Christmas! He is a creative child. He needs all the colors available to develop his artistic potential, she rationalizes.

Christmas is fun. Mom buys a new box of crayons. Junior will love the assortment of colors and Mom will too...they did not have pine-green, mulberry, sepia, bittersweet, wild strawberry, dandelion, and aquamarine crayons when she was a girl!

Binney & Smith Inc. of Easton, Pennsylvania, came up with a new idea in 1986. Plush teddy bears, a little over 6" high, with "Crayola" T-shirts, were a promotional bear offered in the Sunday advertising supplements by the Crayola Company.

The bears were free with proofs-of-purchase and available in several primary colors. Marks: "©1986 Graphics International Inc. K.C. MO 64141, Made in Korea. Reg. PA No. 1043/C2002."

The Burger King Corporation offered the plush Crayola bears as premiums in 1986. A paper tag was added to the bears, with the "Burger King" trademark.

DEL MONTE® DOLLS

**Country Yumkin Fruits —
Del Monte Corp.®, 8"–11",
plush, $10.00 each.**

**Juicy Pineapple — 1983
Country Strawberry — 1989
Lushie Peach — 1982**

**Shoo-Shoo Scare Crow — 1983
Del Monte Corp.®, 14",
plush, $10.00.**

During the 1980's the Del Monte Corporation offered a series of "Country Yumkin®" garden variety dolls. The premium campaign started in 1982 and ended in 1989.

The dolls were made by the Trudy Company and each is well marked with tags sewn in the seams. The tags include the name of the doll, the date, and "Del Monte Corporation.©"

From year to year the qualifiers were changed. The first premiums required enormous amounts of UPCs from Del Monte products (75) in exchange for one free doll. However for five UPCs and $8.95 the dolls were also available.

The first dolls offered in 1982 were Sweetie Pea, Reddy Tomato, Cobbie Corn, and Lushie Peach. Sweetie Pea is 12" tall and made of green plush fabric. His face is light green. Reddy Tomato is 10" tall and made of red plush fabric with green velour feet. Cobbie Corn stands 10½" tall, a yellow and green plush doll. The Lushie Peach doll is the plush fabric in peach tones and green velour feet.

A scare crow, Snappy Bean and Juicy Pineapple were offered in 1983. Shoo-Shoo Scare Crow has a red velour hat, white velour shirt and blue velour pants. The body is peach plush fabric and the clothing is attached. It is 14" tall. Snappy Bean measures 10" and is made of green plush fabric. Juicy Pineapple is also 10" tall. It is a peach colored plush fabric with green velour feet. All of the dolls have black and white plastic eyes and embroidered mouths.

Fluffy Lamb and Cocky Crow were offered in 1984 and the "Yumkin Brawny Bear" was available in 1985.

The 12", plush brown bear with removable blue jeans was a popular premium. He has a yellow hat and a "Del Monte" patch on the bib of the overalls.

In 1989 Del Monte had two premium dolls available, the new Country Strawberry and a renewed offer of Lushie Peach. This time the qualifiers were reduced. Each doll required only two proofs-of-purchase from Del Monte's Yogurt Cup® (a new product) and $1.00 for postage.

Cocky Crow — 1984
Del Monte Corp.®, 10", plush, $10.00.

Fluffy Lamb — 1984
Del Monte Corp.®, 12", synthetic sherpa, $10.00.

Country Yumkin Veggies — Del Monte Corp.®
8"–11", plush. $10.00 each.

Sweetie Pea — 1982
Reddy Tomato — 1982
Cobbie Corn — 1982
Snappy Bean — 1983

Yumkin Brawny Bear — 1985
Del Monte Corp.®, 12", plush, $10.00.

DOLE® CHARACTERS

Bananimals!™ You won't find the word in a dictionary. If you did, the etymology might read like this: [©1989 derived from banana and animal] 1. An animal with banana-like features. 2. An animal with a banana. 3. Any octopod with its eight limbs in the shape and color of a banana. 4. Lizards and reptiles with banana-like features.

The first time I heard about Bananimals was in 1989 when General Foods and the Dole Packaged Foods Company offered four different Bananimals on the back of the Post® Toasties® Corn Flake box.

The Bananabear, Bananapus, Bananarilla, and Bananasaur were pictured in color with the following ad. "Cuddle up to your very own Dole® Bananimal for only $7.95 each plus 1 proof-of-purchase (UPC bar code symbol) from Post® Toasties® Corn Flakes *and* 1 Dole banana sticker. A $15.00 Retail Value! Collect the entire Dole Bananimal Kingdom! Four adorable creatures in all! Each Dole Bananimal is soft, cuddly, plush, huggable, 10" tall, durable, safe, non-toxic, and non-allergenic."

I chose one, the Bananabear, a bright yellow plush animal holding a banana in his arms. The muzzle is black plastic and the eyes are black and white plastic.

The Bananabear is well marked with a tag sewn into a seam: "Dole/BANANIMAL™" is on one side, "©1983 Trudy Toys Co. Inc.," patent numbers, materials and washing instructions are on the other side. A paper tag on the Bananabear's ear identifies the Bananabear as the clown of the Bananimal Kingdom and other personality traits.

The Piney Pals® were the bargain of the day! Blossom and Bamboo are also trademarks of Dole Packaged Foods Company.

These trademark characters are made of quality materials, plush 100% polyester fibers. The bodies are soft gold and the "hair" is green. Black and white plastic eyes are glued to the face. The mouth and brows are embroidered. Blossom is 12" tall and the baby is 4". This delightful pair is destined to stay together. Velcro is stitched to mother's cheek and baby's back.

A tag is sewn to the body of Blossom which reads: "Dole Piney Pals, Blossom & Bamboo, ©Sundara Industries Ltd. 1992, ALL RIGHTS RESERVED, San Francisco, CA U.S.A."

Blossom and Bamboo are a two-piece set that required $5.95 and three proofs-of-purchase or $7.95 and one proof-of-purchase.

Bananabear™ Bananimal — 1989
Dole®, ©Trudy Toys Co., 10", plush, $10.00.

Piney Pals — 1992
Dole®, ©Sundara Industries, 12", plush, $10.00.

A. BANANABEAR™

B. BANANARILLA™

C. BANANAPUS™

D. BANANASAUR™

Cuddle up to your very own Dole® Bananimal™ for only $7.95 each plus 1 proof-of-purchase (UPC bar code symbol) from Post® Toasties® Corn Flakes and 1 Dole® banana sticker. A $15 Retail Value!

Collect the entire Dole® Bananimal Kingdom!! Four adorable creatures in all!

Each Dole® Bananimal™ is
• Soft, cuddly, plush and huggable
• 10 inches tall
• Durable, safe, non-toxic and non-allergenic

Dole Bananimals offer,
Post® Toasties® Corn Flakes. General Foods Corp.

A. B.

Dole PineyPals ORDER FORM

Piney Pals are 10" tall, non-allergenic and child safe. Only $4.95 each plus one UPC as proof-of-purchase from any Dole product! Retail value $18.95. Please send the Piney Pals™ requested below:

	Quantity				Amount
A. Jammin' Joey™	_____	x	$4.95	=	$ _____
B. Luau Lani™	_____	x	$4.95	=	$ _____
			TOTAL ENCLOSED		$ _____

Name _____

Address (no P.O. Box) _____

City _____ State _____ Zip _____

Postage and handling included. Allow 6-8 weeks for delivery. Zip code must be included on your order. Void where prohibited or restricted. Not available in stores, good only in U.S.A. and **WHILE SUPPLIES LAST**. Make check or money order payable to Dole Piney Pals, no cash please. Mail to:

Dole Piney Pals, P.O. Box 8063-D, Clinton, IA 52736

Dole Piney Pals order form.

Dole Piney Pals order form.

DUTCH BOY®

Dutch Boy — Sherwin-Williams®
Doll, 14", cloth, yarn, and mask face, $40.00.
Puppet, 12", vinyl and cloth, $30.00.

The history of the Dutch Boy Paints trademark dates back to 1907. It was first created as an advertising illustration by O.C. Harn.

According to archivist Patricia S. Eldridge, Mr. Harn's specifications called for a drawing of a little Dutch boy, dressed in native overalls, in the act of painting. The illustration was planned because the people of the Netherlands had a worldwide reputation for keeping their buildings white-washed. An illustrator with Dutch ancestry, Mr. Rudolph Yook, made the four original pencil sketches.

Later, when a search was being made for a suitable trademark to represent a group of individual lead manufacturers, the Dutch Boy was chosen. The noted portrait painter, Lawrence Carmichael Earl, of Montclair, New Jersey, was commissioned to paint a portrait for the new symbol.

The model for the Dutch Boy in the painting was a young neighbor of Earl, Michael E. Brady, nine at the time. The legend is, when the posing session was done, Michael received his pay and was so impressed that he wanted to become an artist when he was grown up. He followed his dream, and Michael Brady became famous for his powerful political cartoons.

The blond-haired, blue-eyed boy with wooden shoes, overalls, and a cap has undergone many changes through the years, as the Dutch Boy Paints Company changed advertising agencies and owners. Sherwin-Williams purchased the Dutch Boy name in 1980 from Chicago-based Dutch Boy Inc. In 1987 Sherwin-Williams began using the original design in advertising, after research revealed that customers felt it imparted a feeling of quality. Earl's painting portrays a serious Dutch Boy, hard at work with a paint brush in one hand and the wood paint bucket sitting on the bench beside him.

As a part of the promotional efforts, owners of the Dutch Boy Paints have offered premiums featuring the Dutch Boy.

The doll was a premium of the 50's, and is cloth with a mask face and yarn hair. The clothes are not removable. It measures 14". The 12" puppet was a special gift to anyone who purchased a gallon of Dutch Boy paint in 1956. It has a vinyl head with molded and painted features including the hat.

One day Christian K. Nelson of Onawa, Iowa, became puzzled by a little boy's indecision between a chocolate candy bar and a scoop of ice cream. When questioned, the freckle faced boy replied, "I want 'em both but I only got a nickel."

Nelson had an idea. If he could combine the variables: ice cream, chocolate, and the convenient bar concept, the freckled-faced boy and every other boy could have his scoop of ice cream and the chocolate bar too.

In 1921, Christian Nelson began marketing in the U.S.A. and founded the Eskimo Pie Corporation on the success of the ice cream treat.

Symbols and trademarks were and still are important factors in identification and promotion of products. The Eskimo Pie Corporation chose an image of a happy Eskimo boy for its trademark.

In 1964 the Eskimo Pie Corporation followed the advertising trend of offering a trademark doll to consumers. The premium offer was printed on the back of the ice cream wrapper. For $1.00 anyone could have a delightful Eskimo Boy.

The doll is unmarked but easily recognized with a gold-brown jacket with graphic, red diamonds across the bottom and a white fur-like parka. The pants are black and the boots and gloves are red. The Eskimo Pie Boy is made in the popular style of the 60's and 70's, a cloth doll with printed features and clothes. It was made by the Chase Bag Company. The doll is 15" tall and stuffed with cotton.

Another Eskimo Pie doll, made by the Chase Bag Company, was offered in 1975. It is the same size but there are some changes. The second doll has caricature features that include a broad, line smile and a tongue licking the upper lip. The red jacket is a more vibrant red and "eskimo pie" is printed across the chest in large white letters. The doll's pants are brown and the boots are white.

Eskimo Pie Boy — Eskimo Pie Corp.®, 1964, Chase Bag Co., 15", cloth, $15.00.

Eskimo Pie Boy — Eskimo Pie Corp.®, 1975, Chase Bag Co., 15", cloth, $15.00.

THE GERBER® BABIES

Frank Gerber started the Fremont Canning Company in 1901, located in Fremont, Michigan. Frank's son Daniel joined the company in 1920 and became a major influence on company policy. After Daniel was married and the young couple had their first child, Daniel Gerber had the idea of preparing strained baby food at the cannery. By the end of 1928 Gerber Baby Foods were on the market for 15¢ a can.

The company began using a sketch of a bright looking baby, drawn by artist Dorothy Hope Smith, in advertising. The Gerber Baby was added to the baby food product labels.

The name of the Fremont Canning Company was changed to Gerber Products Company. An advertisement in the June 1936 *Ladies' Home Journal* magazine features the baby, the label and a coupon for a free Gerber Baby. The consumer had a choice of the boy or girl Gerber Baby in exchange for 10¢ and three labels.

If a collector is not familiar with the adorable Gerber Babies, there is no need for concern. The dolls are always well marked. Even the very first cloth dolls left nothing for the imagination, as they hold a can of Gerber baby food in one hand.

In the 1960's the Gerber Babies were made of vinyl and had the molded hair and beautiful open-close eyes. The dolls were wearing a "Gerber Baby" bib and a diaper. The original cost was only $2.00 and 12 Gerber Product labels.

In the 1970's Black and White Gerber Babies were retailed by the Atlanta Novelty Firm. They were available in a range of sizes from 12" to 17". They exhibited a variety of features. Some of them cried "Mama" and others rolled their eyes. Of course, as the dolls became more sophisticated, they were selling at higher prices.

Squeeze dolls are popular too. A 1985 8" vinyl squeeze doll has "I'm a Gerber Kid®" printed on a white apron. Embossed on the bottom: "®1985 GERBER PRODUCTS COMPANY."

A 1989, 14" Gerber Baby has open-close, blue "glass" eyes and "real" lashes. The head, legs, and arms are vinyl and the body is cloth. Embossed on the back of the neck are the markings: "®1989 GERBER PRODUCTS CO. ALL RIGHTS RESERVED."

The doll wears a white christening dress and a Gerber Baby gift set was included. This doll was manufactured by Lucky Industries of New York City, under license.

Gerber Babies are an American tradition and there are some features that have never changed. The molded hair on rubber and vinyl dolls, big round eyes, open mouth and a round face, are indicative of the trademark baby on Gerber Baby food packaging.

Gerber Kid — 1985 Gerber Products Co.®, 8", vinyl squeeze, $15.00.

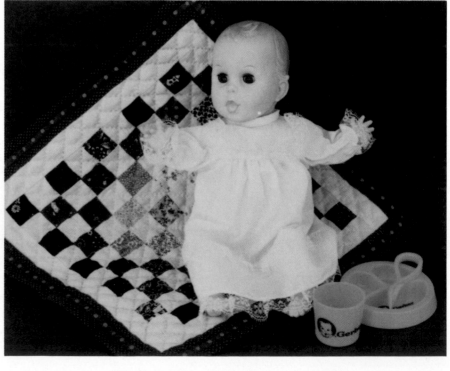

Gerber Baby with gift set — 1989 Gerber Products Co.®, 14", vinyl and cloth, $30.00.

YOU and YOUR BABY

*would enjoy watching
us make strained
vegetable soup*

You yourself, would enjoy seeing how we free you from the drudgery of preparing so many different ingredients. You would be more than satisfied with the plump freshness of our *Home Grown* vegetables—the liberal richness of the added beef stock. And you would see that our methods of cleaning, cooking and straining the vegetables are just the way you would like to have it done—safeguarding in every step, the important vitamins and minerals.

Gerber's Strained Vegetable Soup combines a plentiful supply of *Home Grown* tomatoes, carrots, peas, spinach and celery. Also selected rice, barley and beef. Using only fresh vegetables, we do not season our products, but leave that to you—and the advice of your doctor.

Gerber Baby offer,
Gerber Products Company®
Ladies' Home Journal, June 1936.

Specially
Shaker-Cooked, Too

As you stir food you're heating, we have these foods *shaken* during the cooking process … so heating is even, the foods cook faster, and look and taste *fresher!*

Shaker-Cooked Strained Foods

STRAINED TOMATOES, GREEN BEANS, BEETS, CARROTS, PEAS, SPINACH, VEGETABLE SOUP. ALSO, STRAINED PRUNES AND CEREAL.

Send for this Gerber Baby Doll

Boy Doll in blue—Girl Doll in pink—fine quality sateen, ready stuffed. Send 10c and Three Gerber labels. Specify whether boy or girl doll is desired.

36

GERBER PRODUCTS COMPANY
FREMONT, MICHIGAN

(In Canada: *Grown and Packed by* Fine Foods of Canada, Ltd., Tecumseh, Ont.)

Size of Doll
9 inches high

NAME..

ADDRESS..

CITY..STATE.................

AGE OF BABY.................BOY..........GIRL..........

"Mealtime Psychology", a booklet on infant feeding sent free on request. *"Baby's Book"*, on general infant care, 10c additional.

(This is the enlarged bottom half of the "You and Your Baby" ad at left.)

GINNY® DOLL

Ginny is one of the longest continuously selling dolls on the market. In 1991 Dakin Inc. celebrated Ginny's 40th birthday with a limited edition, "40th Birthday Party Special" doll, complete with a pink taffeta dress, festive pinafore, white knit anklets, pink shoes, white lace-trimmed underwear, and a gold chain necklace with a ruby in the gold heart medallion. The doll also has her own birthday cake, party hat, and wrapped gift.

The Ginny doll was also a promotional doll at the doll convention in 1991, sponsored by *Vogue Doll Revue*.

The birthday doll joins a 1981 Sasson Ginny Doll dressed in Sasson designer jeans. At that time Ginny was a registered trademark of Lesney Products Corporation.

In 1922, Jennie Graves opened the Vogue Doll Shoppe, beginning a tradition of high quality doll manufacturing that continues today in the Vogue Dolls Division of Dakin Inc.

In 1951, Mrs. Graves introduced the Ginny doll, named after her daughter Virginia. Ginny represents childhood in all its wondrous innocence, curiosity and imaginary adventure.

The Ginny dolls are 8" little girl dolls made of vinyl. The 1991 doll has open-close eyes and the 1981 doll has painted eyes. Both dolls have synthetic wigs and they are jointed at the neck, hips, and shoulders...walker dolls they are called. Early dolls of the 50's were non-walkers.

The 40th Birthday Party Special Ginny Doll — 1991 Limited Edition, Dakin Inc.®, 8", vinyl, $50.00. (Doll courtesy of Dakin Inc.)

Sasson Ginny Doll — 1981 Vogue Dolls, Dakin Inc.®, 8", vinyl, $50.00.

"Get a taste of the sweet life at Hershey's Chocolate World." Visitors are invited to visit Hershey's Chocolate World and take free tours to see, first hand, how the delicious milk chocolate candies are made. Browse through the gift shops and feast on the freshest foods at Hershey's Cafe. Share the experience 28 million visitors have already enjoyed at the fantasy land of Hershey, Pennsylvania.

Hershey collectors love to visit "Chocolate Town" and load up on new items to add to their collection. The gift shop offers reproductions of the antique tins with the original corporate symbol, of "Cocoa Babe," which first appeared in 1898.

The Hershey Man® is a favorite trademark treasure. It has a plastic body in the image of a 3" Hershey candy bar. Marks include, "HERSHEY'S"/"MILK CHOCOLATE." Molded on the back, "TRADEMARK OF HERSHEY'S FOODS CORPORATION/ALLEN LEWIS MANUFACTURING CO. LICENSEE."

Hershey's Company began making Hershey's Chocolate Kisses® in 1907. The mouth watering chocolate drop wrapped in foil became a company trademark.

Who doesn't like "kisses?" The famous Kisses were teamed with teddy bears. Older bears were offered in 1980. The larger bear is a 14" teddy bear made of brown and white plush fabric. It has a comical vinyl face and blue t-shirt that is part of the body. The small Hershey Bear measures 7". It was made by the Ideal Toy Company in 1982.

In the 1991 Hershey catalog the 11" "Hershey Kiss Bear" was offered. It is one of the loveliest bears on the market, with fur as soft as mink. It holds a giant Hershey's™ Kiss wrapped in silver lame, and to sweeten the deal, six ounces of candy kisses came with the teddy bear.

Hershey's dolls — Hershey's Foods Corp.®
Hershey Kiss Bear, 11", plush (1991), $30.00.
Hershey's Teddy Bear (blue t-shirt), 14", plush & vinyl (1980), $25.00.
Hershey Teddy Bear (white t-shirt), Ideal Toy Co., 7", plush (1982), $6.00.
Hershey Man, 3", plastic.

GREEN GIANT®

"From the Valley of the Jolly (ho-ho-ho) Green Giant." The largest Jolly Green Giant in the world is 47.5 foot tall and weighs 8,000 pounds. In fact, it is the world's only Jolly Green Giant statue! It has a 48" smile and welcomes tourists along I-90 since July 6, 1979. The statue stands on its permanent home in the Faribault County Fairgrounds in Blue Earth, Minnesota.

Faribault County is known as "Green Giant Country." It began in 1926 when the Blue Earth Canning Company made its first cream style corn. Three years later the Blue Earth Canning Company became a subsidiary of Minnesota Valley Canning and in 1950, the corporation adopted a new name, Green Giant. From then on, our country was invaded by the Jolly Green Giant trademark. The giants appeared on the product labels, in full page color advertising, and TV commercials.

The consumer did not have to read the label to know it was a Green Giant product — this zany character, green like an imaginative alien spaceman, dressed in a green tunic and hat with a leaf pattern, was the identifying symbol of health, happiness, and quality.

In the 60's the Green Giant Company offered Green Giant dolls as premiums. The first Jolly Green Giant is made of green cotton and has lithographed features. The stuffing is shredded foam and the original cost was 50¢ (to cover postage) and three product labels.

In 1974, a new Green Giant and Little Sprout® were offered. The ad was in a Sunday paper comic section. The Green Giant is 28" tall. The facial features are much different than the first doll. It has small round eyes, and a longer line-smile. Little Sprout is only 10½" tall. He has a mischievous expression and white in the eyes. Both dolls were made by the Chase Bag Company and collectors could have the pair for $2.95 and two labels from Green Giant canned or frozen products.

The third doll is made of felt and the green leaf garment is separate from the body. Black and white plastic eyes are glued to the face. Black lines represent the brows and mouth. The felt doll was made by Animal Toys for retail. The PA Registered number is 376.

The fourth doll is the Little Sprout doll, made of vinyl. The head swivels and the body is molded in one piece with outstanding features — leaf tunic and hat, a button nose, and protruding ears. Eyes are painted. The original cost to the consumer for the 6" doll offered as a premium in the 80's was $2.00 and one proof-of-purchase from either Green Giant or Pillsbury® products.

By this time the two companies had merged. Later British Grand Metropolitan took over the company, however they continue to use the well established trademarks.

Other Green Giant collectibles to look for are the 8" flashlight and the jumprope with Green Giant handles. The flashlight character has a handle and switch in the back, glass and bulb under the base. (It could pass for a doll.) Remove the handles from the jumprope and we have two 4" Green Giants!

**Green Giant Dolls — Green Giant®,
(British Grand Metropolitan)
Jolly Green Giant, 1960's, 12", cloth, $10.00.
Little Sprout, 1974, 10½", cloth, $10.00.**

Little Sprout, Green Giant®, 12", felt, $10.00.
Little Sprout, Green Giant®, puppet, $10.00.

Green Giant Assortment — Green Giant®
Plastic flashlight, 1980's, 8", $40.00.
Little Sprout, 1980's, 6", vinyl, $15.00.
Jumprope, 4", $10.00.

JOEY® & JOY®

Joey & Joy — 1990
Joy Cone Co.®, 12½", nylon. $10.00.

Joey and Joy are charming trademark characters owned by the Joy Cone Company. Two dolls were made in their likeness. The dolls are made of nylon fabric and are 12½" tall. Each is endowed with a mop of yellow yarn hair.

The main difference in the features of the brother and sister is the long painted eyelashes on the girl. Both have freckles and a line smile.

Joy Cone Company's marketing division worked with Village Toys to design these dolls, based on the characters that decorate the Joy Cone package. Sneakers, shirt, and jeans are removable on the dolls. They look like "All-American Kids" in the red, white, and blue costumes. Joey could be a baseball player, or a fan with his baseball cap on his head.

Joy and Joey dolls were available in 1990, the first premium doll offer made by the Joy Cone Company. Requirements were 16 UPCs for two free dolls. The number of boy dolls made was 8,328 and the number of girl dolls made was 15,936.

The fact that the Joy Cone Company started in 1918 and is still in existence under a new name is a bit of intriguing history. In a letter from the company, I was informed the company was originally founded by Albert George and was called the George and Thomas Cone Company in 1918. Mr. Thomas was Albert George's cousin.

The company is owned and operated by Albert George's sons, Joe and Fred George, in the 1990's.

Ernie the Keebler Elf — 1974
Keebler Co.®, 6½", vinyl, $25.00.

If I were asked who are the most famous elves in America, I would reply without hesitation...Happy, Doc, Dopey, Sleepy, Bashful, Grumpy, Sneezy, Santa's helpers, and Ernie, the Keebler Elf. In fact Ernie may be the most famous of all!

Yes, Ernie, the cheerful character that playfully promotes Keebler products. He is immediately recognized by his white hair covered with a red hat and always dressed in a white shirt, green jacket, red vest, and yellow trousers.

How does one come to this conclusion when obviously there are no surveys on the subject? My observation reveals Ernie does not hide in a forest of videos. He isn't an elf who comes out only at Christmas time, and he doesn't remain in the pages of a story book waiting for someone to open the door.

Ernie doesn't know what "low-profile" means! He is always in the public eye. Unlike some of the other elves, he is not bashful or grumpy. He never sleeps. Ernie is a hustler, a work-aholic in fact. He stands on every food shelf in America, smiling out at the consumers, encouraging them to buy Keebler cookies and crackers and other goodies.

The Keebler Company made special efforts to attract the younger generation with Ernie dolls and puppets. In 1974 they offered a 6½" vinyl doll with molded features and painted clothing. The head turns. Embossed on the bottom of the feet, "1974 KEEBLER CO."

The offer was on the back of product packaging. Consumers were instructed to send two proofs-of-purchase from Keebler products and $1.00.

KELLOGG® COMPANY DOLLS

Sweetheart of the Corn® — 1970
Kellogg Co.®, 9", vinyl, $20.00.

Above right:
Snap! Crackle! and Pop!® — 1975
Kellogg Co.®, 8", vinyl, $25.00 each.

Snap! Crackle! and Pop!® — 1984
Kellogg Co.®, Talbot Toys Inc.®,
vinyl, 4½", $10.00 each.

Kellogg's Snap! Crackle! and Pop!® have been with us since 1928, when the company started marketing Rice Krispies® and the elves were chosen as trademarks for the cereal. We continue to see them on the packaging, and in advertising.

The first promotional dolls were made 20 years later in 1948. They were cloth dolls to cut and sew. The original cost was 15¢ and one Rice Krispies® box top. According to Kellogg's chronology of dolls offered as premiums, Snap! Crackle! and Pop!® were offered again in 1950, this time in the form of puppets. Five years later, 16" cloth dolls were available to the public. In 1966, prestuffed cloth dolls were offered.

The vinyl dolls, or "Fun Figures," as Kellogg's called them on the back of the Rice Krispies® cereal box, were offered in 1975. They are 8" character dolls that squeak when squeezed. The features are molded and painted. The name of each doll is embossed on the hat and the feet.

In 1984 collectors of advertising characters were invading toy stores, to snatch up a new set of Snap! Crackle! and Pop!®

The three characters are made of soft, flesh-beige vinyl and the features and clothes are painted. They have the typical pointed ears and long nose of the trademark elves but comparing the poseable dolls of

**Toucan Sam® — Kellogg Co.®, Talbot Toys Inc.®,
1984, 4½", vinyl, $10.00.
1994, 4¾", vinyl container, $5.00.**

**Tony the Tiger® — 1980
Kellogg Co.®, 7", hard plastic, $30.00.**

1984 with the 1975 squeak dolls, the colors are slightly different.

Snap! Crackle! and Pop!®, retailed in 1984 by Talbot Toys Inc. are Kellogg licensed products. Surprisingly the only marks the characters have are the names on the hats.

If a collector is lucky enough to find the trio in original boxes, each character is packaged in a 4" x 6" box with a window front. The following trademark notice is on the side of the box: "1984 KELLOGG'S COMPANY, ALL RIGHTS RESERVED/TRADEMARKS OF KELLOGG COMPANY." On the back of the box, "®1984 TALBOT TOYS INC. MADE IN HONG KONG/NEW YORK N.Y. 10010."

William Keith Kellogg and his brother Dr. John Kellogg began experimenting with flaked cereals in 1894. By 1906 John was no longer involved with cereal but W.K. had his own company, the Battle Creek Toasted Corn Flake Company, renamed the Kellogg Company in 1922.

Throughout his life, W.K. and his staff continued to perfect and develop new cereals. Some of them are: All-Bran® (1916); Rice Krispies® (1928); and Kellogg's Corn Pops® (1950).

W.K. Kellogg was ninety-one when he died in 1951. After his demise, the company continued to grow. New products were developed: Kellogg's Frosted Flakes®

(1952); Kellogg's Honey Smacks® (1953); and Kellogg's Special K® (1955), to name only a few.

More sweetened cold cereals were introduced in the 1960's. In 1964 we began seeing the colorful Toucan Sam®, promoting the fruit flavored Froot Loops®.

Froot Loops® are made from a combination of corn, wheat and oat flours and the tiny donut shaped cereal's pastel fruity colors are lemon yellow, strawberry red, lime green and orange.

Kellogg's offered their first pre-stuffed premium in the image of Toucan Sam in 1964.

Froot Loops® continued to be a popular cereal. Two decades later, in 1984, Talbot Toys Inc. marketed the Kellogg trademark Toucan Sam® in several versions. The 4½" doll with poseable wings and head is a favorite. Toucan Sam® was also a finger puppet and a push puppet. Toucan Sam® sat on a raft in the Kellogg's Bath Tub Toy® and the Kellogg Movers® included Toucan Sam®.

Toucan Sam®, is marked under one foot, "®1984 KELLOGG CO./TALBOT TOYS."

In the 1990's Toucan Sam® was offered as a premium on the Kellogg Froot Loops® box. The premium is 5 ounces of blue squeezable paint, with a bright Toucan Sam® head as the lid. It was free with two UPCs and the official order form. The bird and the container are 4¾". Marks, "™ & ©1993 Kellogg Co."

KERNEL RENK®

Steven Renk, president of Renk Seed Company, requested the manufacturing of a doll in the likeness of the Kernel Renk trademark dating back to the 1960's. Dakin, out of Hong Kong, agreed to produce the doll in smaller than usual quantities. Dakin sent Renk several prototypes. One was selected and only 144 dozen dolls were made.

It is an unusual doll with a yellow vinyl head, shaped like a kernel of corn, and a pink soft plastic body. Kernel Renk is 8" tall and has a fringe of white hair painted above his ears. He also has a white manicured mustache and a goatee. The head swivels at the neck, and arms and legs move. There is a cigar in the right hand. "WM F. RENK & SONS CO. INC. 1970" is embossed on the back of the doll's head.

Actually, there was never a Col. Renk, but the seed company officers thought the name, Kernel Renk, would be appropriate, considering the play on words.

Kernel Renk is the only doll the company had but they did have a lot of fun with it. They decided the Kernel needed a mate and a naming contest was held. The winning name for the Kernel's wife was Kornelia! Both logos appeared on promotional items such as pencils, bags, books, and balloons.

The most elaborate Kernel Renk promotional items were the hot air balloons made in the image of the logo. They hovered in the Sun Prairie, Wisconsin, sky over the company headquarters during the summer to advertise the seed company.

After 30 years of service, the Kernel Renk trademark was abandoned in 1991. "It is time for a change," Steven Renk said.

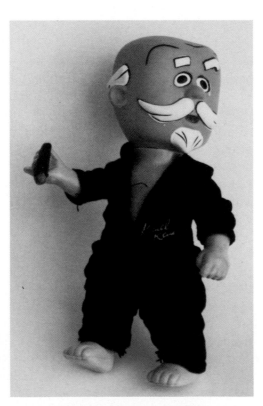

Kernel Renk — 1970
Renk & Sons Co. Inc., 8", vinyl, $20.00.

KOOL-AID® KID DOLLS

Kraft General Foods Incorporated offered the Kool-Aid Kid as a premium in 1989.

The 12½", vinyl doll with the "Kool-Aid Kid™" t-shirt has blond rooted hair and painted, side glancing eyes. Marked on the neck, molded into the vinyl, is "®EEGEE/18 K A 2 — 89/ MADE IN CHINA." There is also a circle with "13" inside the ring, "47" above it and "135 F" below the circle.

In 1993 a Kool-Aid® Barbie® by Mattel was on the Kool-Aid Wacky Warehouse® Free Stuff list. The Collector's Edition Barbie®, the 11½" fashion doll, came with two beach outfits, including a beach bag with the Kool-Aid logo. This prize required 240 Kool-Aid points and postage.

For only 45 points collectors could get an extra pair of shoes and socks, beach shorts, and a blouse.

A Special Edition 35th Anniversary Barbie® Doll celebrating the 35th birthday of Barbie was offered in 1994. The "Kool-Aid Exclusive Barbie" fashion doll has a Malibu tan, sun-streaked hair, and two tropical outfits. The point price is escalating. This one required 300 Kool-Aid points and $1.50 postage and the Wacky Warehouse special order form.

Kool-Aid Kid — 1989
Kraft General Foods Inc.®,
EEGEE®, 12½", vinyl, $20.00.

Kool-Aid
Collector's Edition Barbie — 1993
Mattel®, 11½", vinyl, $20.00.

Kool-Aid
Exclusive Barbie — 1994
Mattel®, 11½", vinyl, $20.00.

MARS FUN FRIENDS®

Did you know M & M's® ("The milk chocolate that melts in your mouth not in your hands") are making history?

According to Mars Inc., during World War II, M & M's chocolate candies were placed in the "C" rations and were a favorite with American soldiers. M & M's were also on the first space shuttle. They have been one of the food options in the shuttle's pantry ever since. In 1984, M & M's chocolate candies was a sponsor of the Olympic Games, helping to develop the next generation of U.S. athletes. M & M's are breaking records, with well over 100 million candies made everyday.

M & M's is a registered trademark of Mars Incorporated. The M & M's were personified by adding stick-figure arms and legs, a happy smile, and eyes. The characters are also registered trademarks of Mars Incorporated. We see them in advertising and collectibles.

In 1988, Mars Inc. added promotional dolls to the advertising efforts. Consumers could have an M & M stuffed toy Fun Friend in exchange for $9.95 and three UPC symbols from the 16 ounce packages of M & M's, either plain or peanut.

Both Plain and Peanut Fun Friends were offered in Sunday supplements and on product packages. The Plain doll is round, like the plain M & M. The Peanut Fun Friend is egg shaped, to resemble the Peanut M & Ms. Plain Fun Friends were available in orange or red plush, and the Peanut style Fun Friends were available in green and yellow. The delightful dolls are 13" tall. The upper half of the body has a cheerful face with an embroidered smile and plastic eyes. A large "m" is appliqued to the front of the body. The offer expired December 31, 1988.

Mars Fun Friends — Mars Inc.®
13", $10.00, ad is from *McCall's*, Christmas, 1988.

RONALD McDONALD® & HAMBURGLAR®

In the United States, McDonald's restaurants stand out from coast to coast. The huge golden arches tower over the landscape, along the freeways and uptown, where real estate sells by the square inch!

According to McDonaldland® descriptions, "McDonaldland is a wonderful, magical place that's anywhere fun resides. It's where Ronald McDonald and all his friends live and have fun. Ronald McDonald represents the fun of McDonald's."

"The McFriendliest Fellow in Town," a personification of the best friend a kid could have, is the unofficial leader of McDonaldland.

The first Ronald McDonald doll, made in 1971 by the Chase Bag Company, is a colorful cloth doll with printed clothes — a gold jumpsuit and red and white shirt. It has a white collar and a zipper with a tab. It measures 16". Some of the later dolls of this style have subtle changes. There are no zipper tabs and the dolls are only 13" tall. All the dolls are well marked with McDonald's Golden Arch trademark. They sold at the restaurants for $1.25.

By 1985, the Ronald dolls were entirely different. They are 15¾" tall, have white mask faces, red yarn hair, a removable gold jumper and red tie shoes. They sold at the restaurants for $12.95.

In 1972, a second character was added to the premium program, a 17" cloth doll by the name of Hamburglar, the resident mischief-maker! Hamburglar is portrayed as a young, fun-loving prankster who happens to love McDonald's Hamburgers and would do almost anything to get one! The traditional costume of Hamburglar includes a black and white striped suit and long orange tie with yellow dots. "McDONALD'S® Hamburglar™" is printed on his back.

Again the 1985 version is new. The doll has a large vinyl head, with features of a mischievous child, and wears a large black plastic hat. This time the doll measures 11".

McDONALDLAND® REMCO DOLLS

Remco evidently had an agreement with McDonald's Systems Inc. in 1976, when they marketed seven dolls in the likeness of trademark characters belonging to McDonald's. These seven trademark characters were used in the TV promotions of McDonald's Systems Inc.

The Remco Company dolls were retailed by Remco and to my knowledge, McDonald's did not sell these dolls over the restaurant counter or use them for promotions.

All of the dolls are 6" to 8" tall, made of vinyl, and can be fully posed. Their heads move up and down and from side to side. Embossed on the back of the bodies is "1976 McDONALD'S SYSTEM INC./REMCO 1976/PAT. PEND."

"Ronald" has red, synthetic hair and wears a removable red and yellow clown suit. Red shoes and red and white socks are molded and painted on the doll.

"Captain Crook®" carries a sword. His carefully molded head features a large nose, tiny black eyes and a mustache. The removable clothes consist of a violet shirt, brown pants and a purple pirate's hat.

"Big Mac®" represents a McDonaldland policeman in his blue suit. The policeman's hat sits on the top of a head shaped like a double hamburger. Eyes and nose are molded and painted on the head.

The brilliant one, "Professor®" has a molded gray beard and wears a white lab coat with tools of the trade in the pockets.

Others to look for are "Hamburglar®," "Mayor McCheese®," and "Grimace®." The Remco "Hamburglar" wears the typical black and white suit and black cape. "Mayor McCheese" is a cheeseburger head atop a doll dressed in striped pants and a vest. He carries his glasses on a string. "Grimace," Ronald's best friend, has a purple plush body and vinyl feet.

Most of the McDonaldland Remco dolls have tiny accessories such as buttons, swords, whistles, glasses. These and the tiny details of their features are part of their charm.

See photos on pages 142–143.

Ronald McDonald — 1980's
McDonald's Corp.®, 15¾", cloth and vinyl, $25.00.

Ronald McDonald — 1971
McDonald's Corp.®, Chase Bag Co., 16", cloth, $10.00.

Hamburglar — 1980's, McDonald's Corp.®
11", vinyl & cloth, $25.00.

Hamburglar — 1972, McDonald's Corp.®
Chase Bag Co., 17", cloth, $10.00.

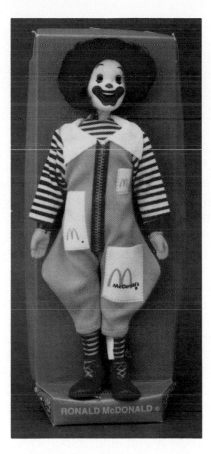

Ronald McDonald — 1976
McDonald's Corp.®, Remco®, 7¾", vinyl, $20.00.

Captain Crook — 1976
McDonald's Corp.®, Remco®, 6", vinyl, $20.00.

Big Mac — 1976
McDonald's Corp.®, Remco®, 6½", vinyl, $20.00.

Professor — 1976
McDonald's Corp.®, Remco®, 6", vinyl, $20.00.

McKEE'S LITTLE DEBBIE®

The McKee Foods Corporation started a tradition in 1985. They offered a 25th Anniversary Little Debbie Doll, made by Horsman. The doll measures 11½". The plastic doll has blond synthetic hair.

A second doll was offered on packages of Little Debbie Snack Cakes in 1990. Quoting from the box:

"This Limited Edition Little Debbie 30th Anniversary Doll has features so warm and radiant you'll almost believe she's real. Made of fine porcelain bisque with natural tones and highlights, the Little Debbie Anniversary Doll is a quality collectible, available for less than half the price you'd pay for a doll of similar quality. Created by the Dynasty Doll Collection, winners of the prestigious Doll's Magazine *Award of Excellence, the Little Debbie Anniversary Doll has poseable arms and legs, and has clear blue Starlight acrylic eyes. From the familiar straw bonnet that tops her curly auburn hair to the fresh white apron that says Little Debbie, this pert charmer is perfect for those just beginning their collection or those adding to their treasures. The Little Debbie 30th Anniversary Doll comes with a Certificate of Authenticity and her own stand. But production is limited, so order today!"*

The 12" porcelain and cloth doll was $15.95 postage and two UPCs. The offer expired December 31, 1990.

A third doll was offered in 1993, the Little Debbie Style Barbie® Doll. This doll captures all the wonderful features of both Little Debbie and Mattel's Barbie Doll.

Harold Matson and Elliot Handler started Mattel in 1945, naming it from letters of both names. Matson sold his share to Elliot and Ruth Handler and they incorporated in 1948. The headquarters were in Culver City, California. The Handlers sold one successful toy after another and introduced the Barbie doll (named after the Handlers' daughter) and Ken® doll (named after the son) in 1959.

Barbie became the most successful brand-name doll ever and 35 years later the 11½" fashion doll, with clothing and accessories, remains a best seller and is often used by other companies as a premium doll.

Clothing for the Little Debbie Barbie resembles the trademark of McKee Foods Corporation, a blue and white checked dress and a sparkling white apron with the "Little Debbie" logo. A straw hat and heels were also included.

Originally requirements were $16.45 and a coupon on Little Debbie Snack Cakes®. The offer expired July 31, 1993. Shipments were made to continental U.S.A. only.

Little Debbie Dolls McKee Baking Co.®

25th Anniversary Little Debbie — 1985, 11½", plastic, $25.00.

30th Anniversary Doll — 1990, 12", porcelain & cloth, $30.00.

Little Debbie Style Barbie Doll — 1993, 11½", vinyl, $20.00.

The Mohawk Carpet Company chose a Native American boy, designed by Walt Disney, as a trademark. They named him Mohawk Tommy, and then gave him full employment.

Mohawk Tommy draws attention to advertising in newspapers and magazines and like other trademarks, identifies a product at first glance. Drive past a Mohawk Carpet business and there's Mohawk Tommy, as big as life in the window. Walk through the store and Mohawk Tommy reminds prospective buyers that Mohawk carpet is available, with his quiet presence.

In 1970 the Mohawk Carpet Company added a trademark premium doll to their promotional efforts and offered each customer a Mohawk Tommy doll with the purchase of Mohawk carpet. This doll was made by the Chase Bag Company. It is a 16" cloth doll with printed features. The tan doll wears a red loincloth and red shoes and is well marked with "Mohawk Tommy" printed on the loincloth and "Mohawk Carpet" printed on the back.

A second Mohawk Tommy was offered in 1991. It is 12" tall and it is made of a tan plush fabric. The doll has a leather-like quiver with real feathers in it.

In 21 years there were many changes in the doll but Mohawk Tommy had not aged as he continued to work for "Mohawk, the first name in Carpet."

Mohawk Tommy — 1970
Mohawk Carpet Co.®, cloth, Chase Bag Co., 16", $10.00.

Mohawk Tommy — 1991
Mohawk Carpet Co.®, 12", plush, $10.00.

MR. PEANUT® DOLLS

Mr. Peanut is still alive and dancing and dolls in his image once again appeared in the 1990's.

The first Mr. Peanut rag dolls were offered in 1967 on the cellophane packages of Planters® Peanuts. At that time the small package was known as "The Nickel Lunch." (Compared to the 45¢ lunch today.)

The premium doll cost $1.00 and two wrappers in the 60's. It measures 21" and has a bright yellow peanut-shaped head and body. The face is printed on both front and back of the doll. There is no cane.

In 1970, a shorter Mr. Peanut was offered. The 18" doll does not have the face printed on both sides. Both dolls were made by the Chase Bag Company.

Another Mr. Peanut doll was offered in 1993 — the Mr. Peanut Holiday Doll, no doubt the most sophisticated premium doll offered. The size alone is impressive! It stands 24" tall. It has a subtle gold, plush peanut body, black velour limbs, cane and hat. Features are embroidered, including the monocle over the right eye. A bright red knit scarf adds a touch of holiday cheer.

This Mr. Peanut premium was featured in a full-page, color ad in Sunday supplements. "Give a Nutty Gift this Holiday Season From Planters," it said. Qualifiers were two proofs-of-purchase from any Planters Nuts 9.5 ounces or larger, the original certificate and $13.99. The offer expired 12/28/93.

The tag sewn to the doll reads: "MR. PEANUT/©1991 PLANTERS LIFESAVERS COMPANY/WINSTON-SALEM NC 27102/ALL NEW MATERIALS/SYNTHETIC FIBERS/MADE IN KOREA/REG. NO. PA 4024."

During 1990 many collectibles were offered on the the small peanut package including the bendie, a bank, cups, and pencils.

Mr. Peanut was available in the 1950's in the form of salt and pepper shakers. One set of 4" shakers are the black and tan peanut man, made of plastic. Mr. Peanut was then the property of Standard Brands Inc.

Smaller shakers, 2¾" tall, were also available at one time. They are plastic and a single color, either red, blue, green or tan.

Cups in the image of Mr. Peanut's head are 4" tall and they were made in tan, green, blue, and red, the same as the single color plastic banks. (See page 40.)

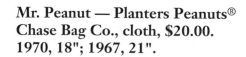

Mr. Peanut — Planters Peanuts®
Chase Bag Co., cloth, $20.00.
1970, 18"; 1967, 21".

Mr. Peanut Holiday Doll — 1991
Planters Lifesavers Company®,
24", plush, $25.00.

Mr. Peanut Assortment — Planters Peanuts®
Mr. Peanut Bendy, 1991, 6", vinyl, $5.00.
Cups, 4", plastic, $10.00.
Salt & pepper, 1950's, 4", plastic, $30.00 a set.

Mr. Peanut — Date unknown
Planters Peanuts®, Scuff Kote,
2¼", plastic, $10.00.

NABISCO'S® DOLLS

When studying company symbols, we discover some of them are ideal for reproduction of three dimensional characters. Take for example the girl with the blue bonnet, featured on the packaging of Blue Bonnet® Margarine. She is a perfect subject for an advertising doll. Consequently, NABISCO Brands Incorporated, the owners of the Blue Bonnet Sue trademark, have added to the American heritage of advertising dolls with several Blue Bonnet Sue® premium dolls.

The oldest Blue Bonnet Sue doll was offered on the package of Blue Bonnet Margarine in 1972. The doll is the common, 8", plastic doll jointed at the neck and shoulders. It has a glued-on blond wig, and blue open-shut eyes. Special attention was given to the costume of the doll. Blue Bonnet Sue is dressed in a bright blue taffeta dress and sunbonnet lavishly embellished with white lace, silver braid and blue satin ribbon.

Blue Bonnet Sue was one of a set of 27 dolls offered by NABISCO Brands Incorporated. This was the "American Heritage Collection" (see ad on page 149) which included such notables as Molly Pitcher, Betsy Ross, Dolly Madison, Martha Washington, and Mary Todd Lincoln.

Blue Bonnet Sue was the first American Heritage doll and the others were offered later, for a cost of $3.00 each, plus any Blue Bonnet "head" from packaging and a coupon.

In 1986, NABISCO Brands Incorporated offered a free Blue Bonnet Sue, a cloth trademark doll with yellow yarn hair and printed features. This is a typical "plaything" for the small children in the family. The doll is dressed in washable clothing, the familiar blue dress and bonnet, and a white apron. If she isn't instantly recognized, "Blue Bonnet Sue" printed on the apron leaves no doubt as to who the doll is. There is also a tag with the doll which says: "MADE EXPRESSLY FOR NABISCO INC.© R. DAKIN & CO. 1986 SAN FRANCISCO, CA. PRODUCT OF KOREA."

In 1989 another doll was offered a "soft and cuddly friend who takes the fright out of the night." This time Blue Bonnet Sue was a large pillow-type doll made exclusively by Springs Industries Incorporated. The pillow doll has the blue dress and bonnet, and sold for $8.74 and 10 brand seals.

Other NABISCO dolls include a 1983 cloth doll representing NABISCO'S pretzels. Mr. Salty® is a brown cloth doll with a collar tied around his neck and a white sailor hat tacked to his head. Facial features are glued on. The doll measures 10".

In 1990 viewers were watching an energetic teddy bear dressed in a fur trimmed jacket with sparkling lapels, advertising NABISCO'S Teddy Grahams® snacks, on prime time TV.

During the same time the Teddy Graham Bear® was appearing on packaging and offered as a premium in Sunday supplements. The beautiful plush teddy bear is almost a foot tall and he was available in exchange for eight brand seals from any Teddy Grahams and $1.00 postage or $5.99 and three brand seals. The offer expired January 31, 1991.

Blue Bonnet Sue — 1972
NABISCO Brands Inc.®, 8", plastic, $20.00.

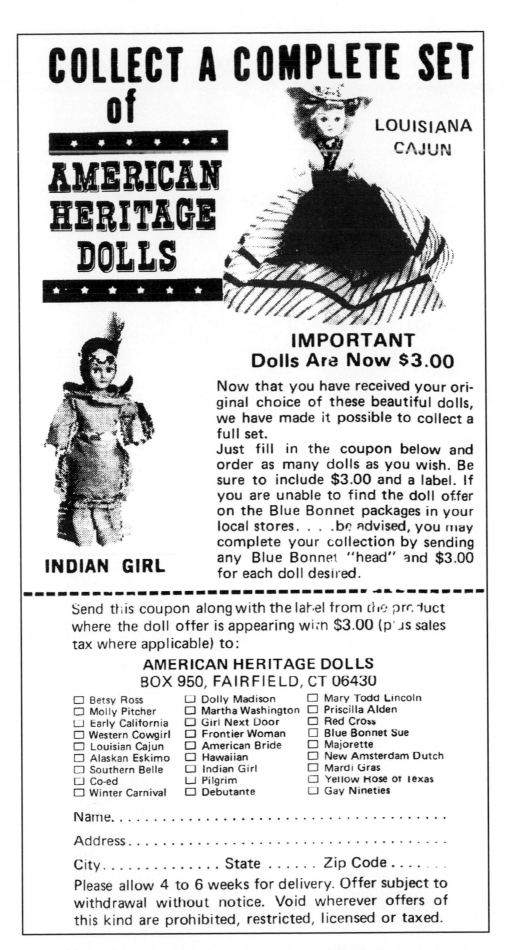

COLLECT A COMPLETE SET of AMERICAN HERITAGE DOLLS

LOUISIANA CAJUN

INDIAN GIRL

IMPORTANT
Dolls Are Now $3.00

Now that you have received your original choice of these beautiful dolls, we have made it possible to collect a full set.

Just fill in the coupon below and order as many dolls as you wish. Be sure to include $3.00 and a label. If you are unable to find the doll offer on the Blue Bonnet packages in your local stores. . . .be advised, you may complete your collection by sending any Blue Bonnet "head" and $3.00 for each doll desired.

Send this coupon along with the label from the product where the doll offer is appearing with $3.00 (plus sales tax where applicable) to:

AMERICAN HERITAGE DOLLS
BOX 950, FAIRFIELD, CT 06430

☐ Betsy Ross
☐ Molly Pitcher
☐ Early California
☐ Western Cowgirl
☐ Louisian Cajun
☐ Alaskan Eskimo
☐ Southern Belle
☐ Co-ed
☐ Winter Carnival

☐ Dolly Madison
☐ Martha Washington
☐ Girl Next Door
☐ Frontier Woman
☐ American Bride
☐ Hawaiian
☐ Indian Girl
☐ Pilgrim
☐ Debutante

☐ Mary Todd Lincoln
☐ Priscilla Alden
☐ Red Cross
☐ Blue Bonnet Sue
☐ Majorette
☐ New Amsterdam Dutch
☐ Mardi Gras
☐ Yellow Rose of Texas
☐ Gay Nineties

Name. . . . .

Address. . . . .

City. . . . . State . . . . . . Zip Code . . . .

Please allow 4 to 6 weeks for delivery. Offer subject to withdrawal without notice. Void wherever offers of this kind are prohibited, restricted, licensed or taxed.

American Heritage Collection, ©1970's NABISCO Brands Inc.®

Blue Bonnet Sue — 1986
NABISCO Brands Inc.®, 11", cloth, $8.00.

Pillow People® Blue Bonnet Sue offer — 1989
NABISCO Brands Inc.®, ©1987 Springs Industries Inc.,
17" x 14" x 6", cloth, $10.00.

Mr. Salty — 1983
NABISCO Brands Inc.®, 10", cloth, $5.00.

Teddy Graham Bear — 1990
NABISCO Brands Inc. ®, 11¾", plush, $20.00.

THE NESTLÉ COMPANY® DOLLS

The Nestlé Company was started by Henri Nestlé of Vevey, Switzerland, and incorporated in 1866. The company's main product, in the beginning, was baby formula and a condensed milk product. In 1929 the Nestlé Company acquired Cailler and Swiss General, companies selling chocolate candy. They introduced the Crunch Bar® in 1938 and Nestlé's Quik® in 1948. Many other companies and products were purchased until Nestlé became one of the world's largest packaged food manufacturers, with factories in Europe, North America, Latin America, the Caribbean, and more.

During the 60's the Nestlé Chocolate Man® was in TV commercials. Once you see him you'll never forget him. He had a great bulbous nose and red hair and mustache. He wore black rimmed glasses, a gold shirt and black lederhosen trousers.

Dolls were made in the likeness of the Nestlé trademark character on TV. The first one is plastic and has a yellow hat molded to his head. The head, arms and legs are jointed. Rooted synthetic fibers represent the mustache. On the back of the neck was the identifying mark, "©1969 THE NESTLÉ CO."

In 1970 another doll, made in the image of the advertising character, was offered. This time it was a Chase Bag Company cloth doll. It measures 15". "The Nestlé Company" is printed on the right foot.

Later premiums offered were in the image of products such as chocolate chips.

How did chocolate chips get in the picture? Here is the story told: "Ruth Wakefield, a proprietress of the Toll House Inn, was experimenting with a favorite colonial cookie recipe. (This was in the 1930's before chocolate chips.) She cut a bar of Nestlé Semi-Sweet Chocolate® into tiny pieces and added them to the dough. The chocolate bits softened to a creamy texture in the baked dessert and Mrs. Wakefield named her delicious discovery the Toll House Cookie!"

With Mrs. Wakefield's permission her recipe was printed on the wrapper of the Nestlé Semi-Sweet Chocolate bar for consumers to enjoy.

In 1939 the Nestlé Company offered the first Semi-Sweet Real Chocolate Morsels®, a convenient chocolate chip in a new package, "the creamiest morsels with the rich, real chocolate taste that made Toll House America's favorite chocolate chip cookie." It was a great success...no cutting, no mess. The homemakers loved the chocolate chip concept.

Nestlé's continued to experiment with more new chips and added Nestlé's Milky®, a light brown, milder chocolate chip; Li'l Bits®, a tiny chocolate chip; P. Nutty® chips; and butterscotch flavored chips.

Historically, new products inspire new promotional dolls. In 1984 the Nestlé Company offered the Morsel Family® dolls as premiums. They are made of plush fabric material in shapes of the product. Each has plastic eyes and nose and removable pieces of clothing. All have sewn-in tags with Nestlé trademark, the Trudy logo, date and materials used.

Nestlé's P. Nutty, a light brown doll with a striped dress, has an embroidered peanut on the front. She is also 19" in circumference.

The little doll is 15" in circumference and she has a pink and white apron and a tiny bow in her hair. She is Morsel Family Baby, Li'l Bit. "She's so tiny, so cute, so sweet, she's impossible to resist! Give her lots of love...and anything sprinkled with Nestlé Little Bits™!"

There is also the Morsel Family's Favorite Uncle. Scotchy® keeps the whole clan happy with one tasty idea: baking his special Oatmeal Scotchies Cookies. This doll is 20" in circumference.

The Morsel Family's Country Cousin, Milky®, wears a blue denim vest and straw hat. The paper tag on him says, "Back to the basics! Milky always says. That's why nothing will do for him but the old fashioned goodness of his favorite homemade candy, Chocolate Almond Bark."

The last doll, Semi-Sweetie®, is the Morsel Family Mom. She is a large doll, 19" in circumference.

The Nestlé Quik Bunny® was a 1985 premium. It is made of soft brown plush fabric and has the big blue "Q" necklace. A Nestlé Quik Bunny cup with long ears for handles was also a premium at that time.

During the 1990's the Nestlé Quik syrup was marketed in plastic bottles in the image of the Quik Bunny and a new Quik Bunny cup was available. It will be interesting to see what will be next.

See photos on pages 152–153.

Nestlé's Chocolate Man — 1969
The Nestlé Co.®,
12½", plastic, $40.00.

(Clothes in picture are reproductions).

Nestlé's Chocolate Man — 1970
The Nestlé Co.®, Chase Bag Co.,
15", cloth, $15.00.

Morsel Family Dolls — 1984
The Nestlé Co.®, 15" to 20" in circumference, plush, $10.00 each.
P. Nutty, Li'l Bit, Scotchy, Milky, and Semi-Sweetie.

Nestlé Quik Bunny — 1985
The Nestlé Co.®, 12", plush, $12.00.

Also: plastic cup (1980's), blue plastic cup (1990's), $7.00;
plastic Quik Bunny container, $6.00; and 6" Bendy (1990), $9.00.

NORTHERN TISSUE® DOLLS

Have you noticed the little girls on the packaging of the Northern Bathroom Tissue?

The James River Corporation offered premium dolls in the image of the trademark girls on the package. The first three required the girl's faces from three packages for each doll ordered plus $10.95. (The official mail-in order forms were in the package).

The Northern Dolls are delightful gifts and collectibles. They have painted features including freckles and smiling mouths with teeth. They all have rooted synthetic hair and vinyl heads and hands. The bodies are flesh-colored cotton with white cloth shoes sewed to the legs. The dolls are 16" tall.

The first premium doll has strawberry-blond hair and wears a yellow dress with white lace trim. Inscribed on the back of the head is the marking, "NORTHERN™ DOLL/©JAMES RIVER CORP. 1986."

A second doll was offered in 1988. The offer was good until March 31, 1989. The consumer had the option of participating in the U.S. Marine Corps Reserve Toys for Tots program. A toy would be donated to a deserving child in your behalf for filling in the certificate.

This doll had ponytails tied with yellow ribbons and she is wearing a green jumper and yellow print blouse. Marks on the back of the head are "NORTHERN™ DOLL/©JAMES RIVER CORP. 1988."

The third Northern Tissue doll was offered at the same cost as the two previous dolls. This doll has blond braids and blue eyes and is ready for bed in a white flannel nightgown, trimmed with eyelet and blue ribbon. Marks inscribed on the back of the dolls head are almost the same with only the change of date: "NORTHERN™ DOLL/JAMES RIVER CORP. 1990."

The James River Corporation offered a black doll and another white doll in 1993. The black doll has curly pony tails, a smiling mouth with teeth and tiny dimples. Pink PJs cover her soft brown, cloth body. The booties are white. Marks inscribed on the back of the dolls head: "NORTHERN™ DOLL/JAMES RIVER CORP. 1993."

The white doll has red hair and a white night gown. The requirements for each doll was $11.95 and two UPCs from any Quilted Northern bathroom tissue packages.

Northern Tissue Dolls — 1986, 1988, 1990, 1993
James River Corp.®, 16", vinyl and cloth, $20.00 each.

The Pepsi-Cola trademark was registered in 1903, five years after Caleb D. Bradham invented Pepsi. Bradham struggled with his Pepsi company for the next 20 years and then sold the company to the Loft Candy Company.

The Pepsi-Cola Company emerged from this transaction. New ideas were developed. The beverage was sold in cans. Slogans, such as "Be Sociable, Have a Pepsi," by company president Alfred N. Steele, became part of advertising in 1950.

By 1963 we were "The Pepsi Generation!" In 1965 the Pepsi-Cola Company was renamed PepsiCo Inc. Somewhere in all the activity Santa Claus took part in progress. The dolls were provided to merchants for advertising displays.

The Seven-Up Company followed the same trend. Seven-Up had come a long way. It was first named Bib-Label Lithiated Lemon-Lime Soda by owners Charles Grigg and Edmund Ridgway. One smart move was shortening the name to 7-Up® and like other beverage companies they developed new slogans: "7-Up Likes You" (1930's) and "Nothing Does it Like Seven-Up" (1960's). Seven-Up has been the "The Uncola®" since 1970.

Trademark characters and Santa Claus promoted the product. In the 50's a cartoon bird character, Fresh-Up Freddie®, was popular. More recently the 7-Up Spot trademark is used but we continue to see Santa Claus at work. Store owners keep the old promotional dolls and bring them out during the Christmas season. Store owners tell me promotional items can be obtained but they are no longer provided free by the companies.

The "Pepsi®" Santa Claus is recognized by the logo on the belt buckle. The doll is made of a plush fabric and has plastic eyes. It has shredded foam stuffing and stands 20". The tag on the doll says it was made by Animal Fair Inc. of Eden Valley, Minnesota. Date is unknown.

The "7-Up" Santa Claus has a mask face with a synthetic beard. The jacket and hat is velvet trimmed with fake fur. This doll is a form of wire and cardboard covered with the red clothing. The 7-Up® logo serves as a belt buckle. It is 24" tall. Date is unknown.

Photos continued on page 156.

"7-Up on the Spot" is a 1988 doll, with suction cups, made of red and black plush fabric and white cotton. It is 6" tall and made by the ®Commonwealth Toy & Novelty Co. Inc. Spot and Spot characters are trademarks identifying products of the Seven-Up Company in Dallas, Texas.

The Spot key chain marks, molded on back, are "7-UP Spot™ is a registered trademark of the Seven-Up Company. 1991. Made in China." It is 2½", and made of red, white, and black PVC.

(Pepsi and 7-Up Santa display dolls are courtesy of the Market, in Arlington, Iowa.)

Pepsi Santa — Date unknown
PepsiCo®, Animal Fair Inc.®, 20", plush, $50.00.

7-Up Santa — Date unknown
Seven-Up Co.®, 24", various materials, $50.00.

7-Up Spot — Seven-Up Co®
7-Up on the Spot® doll with suction cups, Commonwealth Toy & Novelty Co. Inc.®, 1988, 6", $5.00.
Spot® bendy key-chain, 1991, 2½", PVC, $5.00.

For over a quarter of a century, the Doughboy has been one of the nation's most popular advertising characters. You know who I mean...the dough-like character with the bright blue eyes and a giggle. He always wears a chef's hat and a scarf around his neck and that is all!

Ever since Rudy Perz, a creative director at the Leo Burnett Company, created the Doughboy in 1965, we have seen this Pillsbury trademark on products of all kinds: cookies, sweet rolls, biscuits, pizza crust and pie crust. The Doughboy makes appearances in color ads in "slick" magazines and TV.

His cheerful giggle and energy-packed animation are characteristics consumers don't forget.

Like other ad dolls there is a story behind the Doughboy. It began in 1930 with a baker in Louisville, Kentucky. Lively Willoughby was his name. Lively liked to make biscuits but he did not know what to do with the unbaked biscuits, so he wrapped them in foil and packed them in cardboard tubes and put them in the icebox. When Lively took the biscuits out of the icebox to bake them the compressed dough turned the kitchen into a shooting gallery! The tubes were exploding with such force that biscuits were hanging from the light fixtures. Lively, his wife, and son were getting out step ladders and scraping the sticky stuff off the walls and ceiling with a putty knife!

I don't have the details of how Lively did it but eventually he made the process work and sold the idea to Ballard and Ballard Flour Company. Pillsbury acquired the Ballard and Ballard Flour Company in 1952 and the refrigerated dough concept was part of the deal. But consumers raised on the "bake it from scratch" methods were not always aware of fresh home baking with refrigerated dough, and they had to be told. Pillsbury chose to use the Doughboy as the spokesperson.

Shortly after the Pillsbury Doughboy was born, a new advertising doll was made available to the public. The first doll was ready-made by the Chase Bag Company of Reidsville, North Carolina. It is a 12½" cloth doll. New dolls were added later — the Poppin' Fresh Doughboy, and Doughboy's best friend, Poppie Fresh. These vinyl dolls in the trademark likeness were first available in 1971. In 1990 they were available to the public again. "Your very own 7" Doughboy to squeeze and poke," the ad said in a Sunday paper coupon offer by the Pillsbury Company.

Another doll was offered to celebrate the 25th birthday of the Doughboy. This doll is a 13" plush doll with a white cotton baker's hat and white cotton scarf. The tag reads, "POPPIN' FRESH PLUSH DOLL — 25TH BIRTHDAY SPECIAL EDITION" — THE PILLSBURY CO. — 1990 DAKIN INC." It was available for $10.00 and proofs-of-purchase.

Pillsbury Dolls — The Pillsbury Co.®
Pillsbury Doughboy, 1960's & 1970's, 12½"–13", cloth, $12.00.
Poppie & Poppin Fresh, 1970's & 1990's, 7", vinyl, $10.00.
Pillsbury Doughboy salt and pepper shakers, 1980's, 3½", ceramic, $20.00.
Pillsbury Doughboy, 1990, 13", plush, $15.00.

PROCTER & GAMBLE DOLLS

In 1837 William Procter and James Gamble, brothers-in-law, established the firm of Procter & Gamble. It developed into one of the nation's biggest advertisers, and aggressive, inventive advertisers they are. The famous line "Ivory soap will float...99 44/100 per cent pure" is theirs.

The Cincinnati, Ohio, company has an assortment of beauty care products, fragrances, health-care and cleaning aids. Some of the cleaning products are Spic and Span® (1926), Ivory Snow® (1930), Tide® (1946), Comet® (1956), Ivory Liquid® (1957), Downy® (1960), Cheer®, Oxydol®, Dash®, and Bold®.

Part of the marketing plan has included offering premiums with the product. No UPCs to clip, register tapes to save, coupons to fill out and no cash requirements! What you see is what you get and consumers were delighted!

In 1960 dolls were wrapped with King-Sized All-Temperature Cheer. One doll to a box, in a cellophane sack, with a loop for easy display on a peg board or in a cupboard. The only identification for this premium doll is the sticker on the bag, "FREE DOLL MADE IN HONG KONG with purchase of King Size Cheer."

The body and limbs are made of a fragile plastic, easily dented or punctured. The head is a heavier vinyl material with rooted synthetic hair and painted features. Both Black and Caucasian 10" dolls were available in a variety of costumes always including white boots.

The year Walt Kelly died, 1975, the Pogo characters were included in the packaging of some of the cleaning products such as Spic and Span. The figures are 4 to 6" tall. They have heads that will move. Each doll is made from a specific color of vinyl and features are painted. Beauregard Montimingle Bugleboy, the gold hound, has a red and white sweater. Howland Owl is a tan bird wearing white rimmed glasses. A brown Porky Pine has a black and orange hat. Pogo Possum, white, wears a gold hat and black and gold shirt. Two other characters are green Albert Alligator and Churchy LaFemme the turtle. Character name and "©1969 WALT KELLY" is incised on each doll.

**Cheer Doll — 1960
Procter & Gamble®,
10", plastic, $20.00.**

**Pogo Characters — ©1969 Walt Kelly, 4"–6", vinyl, $10.00 each.
Beauregard Montimingle Bugleboy (gold hound), Albert Alligator, Howland Owl, Churchy LaFemme
(turtle), Porky Pine (orange hat), and Pogo Possum (gold hat). Courtesy of Muriel Green.**

QUAKER OATS® DOLLS

The history of Quaker Oats dates back to 1873. It was started by John and Robert Stuart as North Star Oatmeal Mills. In 1881 the name was changed to the American Cereal Company. Twenty years later, Quaker Oats was incorporated. The headquarters is in Chicago, Illinois.

Some of the products with the Quaker Oats label are Quaker Oats oatmeal, corn meal, grits, pearled barley, bran, farina, pettijohns, pancake mix, and ready-to-eat cereals.

It was 1960 when the Quaker Oats Company added ready-to-eat cereal to their line of products and Cap'n Crunch® was a new trademark for the cold cereals.

The Cap'n Crunch trademark doll was produced and offered in 1978. The doll is 15½" and was available for $5.95 and two labels. It is made of velour.

In April of 1990 the Cap'n Crunch Plush Toy offer was on the boxes of Crunch Berries® made by Quaker Oats. The doll is 18" tall and made of "huggable soft material." It was available in exchange for $14.00 and the official mail-in certificate from the cereal box.

Cap'n Crunch has a large, blue captain's hat with a gold "C" on it. His eyes are plastic, painted blue. The captain has pink arms and face, a white body (trousers), black boots and blue jacket with gold trim.

In 1992 the "Where's Waldo?®" dolls were promotions for the Quaker Oats Company LIFE® cereal. You could cut out the coupon and save $3.00 on any of the three dolls at your nearest retailer. The LIFE packaging is loaded with fun and games. The back of the box features a "Where's Waldo" picture and a challenge to find Waldo.

Waldo was the world's most famous missing character in 1992. He was created by Martin Handford and first appeared in *Where's Waldo?*, published by Little, Brown and Company in 1987. According to a press release sent by Mattel Toys, the books are printed in 22 countries and 16 different languages. In America, *The Great Waldo Search* was on the *New York Times* best selling list for a year.

Handford had a unique idea for the age-old, favorite kids game, Hide-and-Seek. Waldo is "drawn" to crowds and it is the reader's challenge to find him. He may be hiding in a forest with hundreds of "nasty-nasties," or on a battlefield, or among ferocious red dwarfs, or unfriendly giants, and other objects of Handford's fantasy world imagination.

What are "Waldo Watchers" looking for? He could be the boy next door (almost). Waldo always wears the same thing, a red and white striped t-shirt, blue jeans and brown "work" shoes. A mop of brown hair tumbles from beneath a red and white stocking cap and his "pin dot" eyes are accented with white lenses in round, black-rimmed glasses. All predictions of Waldo's success came true when he became an animated character and premiered on TV September 14th, 1991. Some called Waldo a "cultural phenomenon."

Waldo and his friend Wenda® are 18" tall and have vinyl heads, hands, and feet. They are poseable cloth dolls made by Mattel Inc. Woof® is plush fabric. All the characters are copyright of Martin Handford 1991. (Waldo dolls are courtesy of Mattel.)

Waldo, Wenda, & Woof — 1991
Martin Handford®, Mattel,
Waldo & Wenda, 18",
vinyl & cloth, $20.00 each.
Woof, $10.00.

**Cap'n Crunch — 1990
Quaker Oats Company®,
18", plush, $20.00.**

**Cap'n Crunch — 1980's
Quaker Oats Company®, 3" & 2", vinyl toys, $3.00 each.**

THE RAID BUG®

Raid Bug — 1992
S.C. Johnson & Sons Inc.®, 9", plush, $15.00.

This bug won't bug anyone! I found him in the *Des Moines Register* Sunday advertising supplement, July 12, 1992. It was printed in color along with an imaginative ad. It said,

> "*RAID PRODUCTS kill roaches wasps, hornets, fleas, ants, flying insects and more. If you have a bug problem, RAID is the answer. It doesn't toy with bugs. It kills bugs dead.*
>
> *And after you've knocked the stuffing out of bugs, send away for a stuffed toy modeled after the famous Raid cartoon bugs. All it takes is a RAID proof-of-purchase and $7.35.*"

Collectors had almost six months to chase this bug down. The deadline for the Raid Bug offer was December 31, 1992. The promotion was also in store displays.

According to Julie Richardson, Assistant Brand Manager for S.C. Johnson & Sons Inc., the makers of Raid products, the Raid Bug was first used in advertising in 1956. The cartoon-like characters were designed by Hollywood animators and the voice of the Raid Bug on TV was Mel Blanc.

The Raid Bug used in the last 20 years in advertising was designed by Don Pegler. It was designed with the original Raid Bug in mind but some changes were made.

In 1987 a three dimensional Raid Bug was produced for internal company use. It was a premium given to sales people in the company. The number is unknown.

The new Raid bug is a "mean" looking roach with big, crossed eyes, and a tuft of black hair on its head. The body measures 9", but if you stand the bug up he will easily measure 14". The majority of the bug is made of green plush polyester, and a darker green felt-like fabric is used for the wings. Only 16,000 Raid Bugs were made for this promotion exclusively for S.C. Johnson & Sons Inc., by Soft Paws Inc.

S.C. Johnson & Sons Inc., in Racine, Wisconsin, was founded in 1886 by Samuel C. Johnson. Home care products include Johnson Wax®, Clean 'n Clear®, Glade®, Glo-Coat®, Pledge®, Shout® and several others. In 1956, Raid was the first indoor/outdoor insecticide and soon after they introduced Off!®, an insect repellent.

Diversification in the 1970's included several personal care products such as Edge®, the shaving gel, and Agree® shampoo and conditioner.

S.C. Johnson & Sons Inc. is in the United States and 46 other countries.

William Booth (1829–1912), an English revivalist, established the Salvation Army in 1865. The international organization was designed for religious and philanthropic purposes.

General William Booth, a former Methodist minister, presented the Gospel to the people of the East End slums in England and organized the Christian Mission. Thirteen years later the name of the organizations was changed to Salvation Army.

The Salvation Army was established in the United States in 1880. Now it is in 85 countries and there are 25,000 officers (ordained ministers) of the group.

Salvation Army undertakes a number of causes. Providing hospitals for unwed mothers is one major endeavor. Building low-cost lodging for the needy, and offering nursery care for working mothers, family work programs, and fresh air camps for boys all require hours of manpower and more money than is ever available.

The street corner musicians, ringing the bell, singing and pleading for funds for the needy, remain on the American scene, especially at Christmas.

A national publication of the Salvation Army, *The War Cry*, began its 115th year in 1995. The magazine is published biweekly with each issue averaging over 500,000 copies.

For more information on the organization, write the Salvation Army National Publications, 615 Slaters Lane, Alexandria, VA 22313.

The 11½" Salvation Army Lass is made of rubber. The clothes were molded and painted. Each character has a white shirt with the Salvation Army emblem on the front, a shield with a white stripe cut diagonally across. Some are green and some are red. The beanies on their heads match the color of the emblem. A squeaker toy is in the beanie. Date is unknown but believed to be in the 1920's.

Salvation Army Lass — Date unknown
Salvation Army Emblem, 11½", rubber, $35.00.

SNUGGLE® BEARS

According to Lever Brothers public relations coordinator Sheryl B. Zapic the "Snuggle" tradename first appeared on the box of Snuggle Fabric Softener® in Germany in 1970. It wasn't until 1983 that Snuggle Fabric Softener was introduced in the United States.

At this time, a well-known puppeteer, Kermit Love, designed the animated Snuggle Bear and literally brought the trademark to life. Snuggle Bear became a celebrity as he appeared on television commercials.

Snuggle Bear is cuddling up to the "Snuggle" logo on the packaging and in advertising in women's magazines. One early ad in *McCall's* magazine pictures Snuggle Bear wrapped in a red Turkish towel and printed below: "Now I get everything fresher than ever before. And because it's me, your wash will be oh-so soft and static free. Remember, only Snuggle Fabric Softener gets your whole wash as soft as me."

Now tell me, who wouldn't want to try this product? The kids love Snuggle Bear...and Mom and Dad love the towels after they have tumbled with Snuggle sheets!

Snuggle Bear was getting loads of attention and the company soon offered a small Snuggle Bear premium. In 1983 the Snuggle Bear was 6" tall, a light brown bear, perfect for the little people in the family.

Lever Brothers offered Snuggle Bear again. The coupon was in the "Surf & Snuggle Bear offer" in the Sunday paper advertising supplement. A collector could have a 14" Snuggle Bear for $4.95, a UPC from both Snuggle Fabric Softener and a 64 ounce bottle of Surf. The cash register receipt was also required.

This premium is a soft and cuddly, creamy white sherpa bear with a beige muzzle and foot pads. The bear has black and brown plastic eyes and a black plastic nose. The Snuggle Bears are well-marked. They have sewn-on cloth tags with "Snuggle™/1986 LEVER BROTHERS COMPANY/ALL RIGHTS RESERVED" and on the back of the tag, "RUSS BERRIE & CO INC./™ OAKLAND, NJ/ALL NEW MATERIALS/SYNTHETIC FIBERS/K69 Pa. Reg. No. 259/Item No. 3146 MADE IN KOREA 8701."

Snuggle Bears — Lever Brothers®
Russ Berrie & Co. Inc.,
(1986), 14", plush, $20.00.
(1983), 6", plush, $10.00.

"Try the new anywhere, anytime treat from Swiss Miss. You'll find Swiss Miss Pudding Sundaes®, along with all our great tasting puddings, in the dairy case. Because they are made from the freshest ingredients, like fresh skim milk."

Accompanying the 1978 *Family Circle* ad was a picture of an opened carton of creamy chocolate Swiss Miss Pudding Sundae and a dairy maid dressed in a blue jumper and white apron. She has blond hair, braided neatly and tied with red ribbons. This is only one of the numerous ads the Swiss Miss has appeared in since 1960 as the spokesperson for the Swiss Miss products of Beatrice/Hunt Wesson Incorporated.

In 1978 the company offered a 17" cloth doll in the likeness of the trademark. The doll was made by Product People Incorporated. The doll has yellow yarn hair, done up in braids, and painted blue eyes. She has a blue removable jumper with the crisp white apron. A cloth tag reads, "Swiss Miss™ ©1977 BEATRICE FOODS CO."

A collector could have this doll for $4.50 and one proof-of-purchase from Swiss Miss Hot Cocoa Mix®.

A second trademark doll offer in 1990 was on Swiss Miss Hot Cocoa Mix and expired April 30, 1991. The doll cost $3.99, plus 75¢ postage and two proofs-of-purchase.

The 1990 Swiss Miss is 13½" tall. She has a soft cloth body and the head is made of vinyl. She looks alive with blushing cheeks and open/shut eyes. She has the same hair-do and the braids are made of yarn and tied with red ribbons. The white "stockings" are actually the legs, and black shoes are sewed to the legs. Like the trademark she has a blue jumper, white blouse and apron. Look closely — embroidered flowers and "Swiss Miss" decorate the new apron. On tag sewn to body, "SWISS MISS/SMITH MARGOL/FABRIC CONTENT/65% POLYESTER 35% COTTON/MADE IN CHINA."

Swiss Miss — 1977
Beatrice Foods Co.®, 17", cloth, $15.00.

Swiss Miss — 1990
Beatrice Foods Co.®, Smith Margol,
13½", cloth and vinyl, $15.00.

**Trix — General Mills Inc.®
(1977), 8½", vinyl, $35.00.
(1986), plush, $10.00.**

**Fruit Brute and Count Chocula —
General Mills Inc.®
1975, 7½", vinyl, $35.00.
1975, 8", vinyl, $35.00.**

"Trix are for Kids…and collectors!" General Mills Inc. started marketing Trix cereal in 1954. Since that time consumers have become acquainted with Trix Playmate®, the logo for the cereal and a General Mills trademark.

For those of you that have never tried Trix, it is a cold cereal made basically from yellow corn meal. The corn puffs literally melt in your mouth.

Consumers have witnessed several changes in the Trix Playmate logo. On the 1960 package, the rabbit appears to be a cloth character with squared off ears. Only a part of his body is used as he sits eyeing the bowl of fruit-flavored corn puffs. In 1961 Trix Playmate wears roller skates as he tips a spoonful of cereal from a glass bowl. Only the head of Trix Playmate is shown in 1967 and he has the broadest smile ever!

An 8½" vinyl Trix Playmate toy was offered in 1977 for a premium. "Trix" incised on the left heel, "General Mills Inc. REG.™," on right heel.

In 1986 the Trix logo is still on the front of Trix Cereal boxes, with a picture of a plush rabbit.

"Now…Your very own TRIX Rabbit!" the box reads. For one UPC and $11.95 the consumer could have a high quality plush, washable Trix Rabbit. "Trix" is embroidered on the bottom of the left foot. The offer expired June 30, 1987.

In 1975 General Mills offered other dolls. Fruit Brute®, a wolf with striped overalls representing Fruit Brute presweetened cereal, is a vinyl squeeze toy 7½" tall.

Another squeeze toy, made of vinyl, 8" tall, represents General Mills Count Chocula® Cereal, the "Chocolate Flavored Frosted Cereal." The original cost for both dolls was one box top and $1.00 for postage and handling.

TROLLS

An April 1992 article in *Playthings* magazine prompted me to predict trolls would be popular advertising characters in the near future. By all reports trolls were a hot item on the market.

"She collects trolls. Now there's a special one for her warm hugs." This was the "Just say it with Russ" advertisement featuring a "special" troll with pale pink hair and a darling pink dress, complete with a tam to match, featured in *Playthings*. The same ad was placed in *People, Time, Good House-Keeping, McCall's, Redbook, Woman's Day, Glamour,* and *Sassy* magazines.

An Atlanta, Georgia, merchant attributed the popularity of trolls in her area to the heavy advertising on TV. Boys and girls both are fascinated with the creatures of the fantasy world and they caught on like wildfire.

A troll is not just a troll, see one and you haven't seen them all. Trolls are short and tall from 1½" to toddler sizes. There are troll kids and adults, doctors, nurses, clowns, and Santa. We see trolls with pointed ears, round ears, little hair and lots of hair. They may have painted eyes or plastic eyes. Some trolls have four fingers and four toes and "jewels" in the navel.

Kraft offered a Kool-Aid® Troll made by RUSS in 1993. The troll was offered on the "Free Stuff" Wacky Warehouse® form and required 75 Kool-Aid Points and 90¢ postage.

The troll measures 4" from its feet to the top of the head. Add another 3" of hot pink hair and he is a grand total of 7". The vinyl body is molded in one piece and includes four tiny toes on each foot and four fingers on each hand. Facial features include a flat nose and a wide smile. Sparkling brown plastic eyes are glued into molded eye sockets. Another identifying feature of the Kool-Aid® trolls is the white cotton t-shirt with blue and black "Kool-Aid" printed on the front. Both t-shirt and pink print shorts are removable.

Kool-Aid Troll — 1993
Kool-Aid, RUSS, 4", vinyl, $8.00.

A Minute Maid® Troll also made by RUSS, 7" tall with magenta hair, dressed in a Minute Maid shirt, was offered on the package of Minute Maid, a product of the Coca-Cola Company. The eyes are brown plastic with black pupils. The troll is made of vinyl.

The qualifiers for this prize were four UPCs cut from the bottom of the cardboard overwraps of Minute Maid In-The-Box 9-packs along with 50¢ postage and the mail-in certificate on the overwrap. The offer expired December 31, 1993.

Russ Berrie and Company Trolls all have "RUSS®" embossed under one foot and "CHINA" under the other.

During March 1993, Wal-Mart management offered a free Treasure Troll® with a purchase of a "Kid's Meal." They are 1½" tall plus 1½" of hair. A choice of either the troll on a necklace or a pencil was available. These trolls are trademarks of the Ace Novelty Company, copyright 1991 and made in China.

May 23, 1993, Sunday supplements carried an ad for Spray 'n Wash Tough Stain Remover® for Laundry, a Dow Brands product. For two proofs-of-purchase and 75¢ a customer could get a Pizza Troll. The trolls wear a white baker's hat and shirt, blue pants, and a red and white checked apron. A replica of a pizza is fastened to one hand with a rubber band. The only mark on the trolls is "MADE IN CHINA" on the bottom of one foot.

The trolls offered by the Burger King Corporation in 1993 have, molded on the back of each, "BURGER KING/KIDS CLUB™" and below that is a name. Snapy, Jaws, I/Q, and Kid Vid are four. These characters have molded and painted clothes and the heads are a "glow in the dark" vinyl. Each measures 3" plus the hair. Molded on the bottom of one foot is "®1993 BURGER KING CORP."

During the summer of 1993 Sunline Brands Inc. offered Tangy Taffy® Trolls on special marked packages of Tangy Taffy. They required two UPCs and $1.50 postage and handling. The trolls are 6" tall including the hair and each wears denim shorts and a Tangy Taffy trademark shirt. They have "MADE IN CHINA" on one foot, no other marks.

Minute Maid Troll — 1993
Coca-Cola Co., RUSS,
7", vinyl, $5.00.

Treasure Trolls — 1993
Wal-Mart, Ace Novelty
Co., 1½", (on pencils),
vinyl, $3.00.

Pizza Troll — 1993
Dow Brands, 6", vinyl, $5.00.

Snapy, Jaws, I/Q, and Kid Vid — 1993
Burger King Corp.®, 6", glow in the dark vinyl, $5.00.

Tangy Taffy Troll — 1993
Sunline Brands Inc., 6", vinyl, $5.00.

BIBLIOGRAPHY

Anderton, Johana Gast. *The Collector's Encyclopedia of Cloth Dolls*. Lombard, Illinois: Wallace-Homestead Book Company, 1984.

Dotz, Warren. *Advertising Character Collectibles*. Paducah, Kentucky: Collector Books, 1993.

Glim, Esop. *How Advertising is Written and Why*. New York, New York: McGraw-Hill Book Company Inc, 1945.

Hake, Ted. *Hake's Guide to Advertising Collectibles*. Radnor, Pennsylvania: Wallace-Homestead, 1992.

Hoover, Gary, Art Campbell, Patrick Spain, *Hoover's Handbook of American Business — 1992*. Austin, Texas: The Reference Press Inc., 1992.

Kleppner, Otto. *Advertising Procedure — Seventh Edition*. Englewood Cliffs, New Jersey: Prentice-Hall Inc., 1979.

Kovel, Ralph and Terry. *Kovel's Advertising Collectibles Price Guide*. New York: Crown Publishers Inc., 1993.

Longwith, John. *The Spark of Enterprise*. Cleveland, Tennessee: Magic Chef Inc., 1988.

Mendenhall, John. *Character Trademarks*. San Francisco, California: Chronicle Books, 1990.

Packard, Vance. *The Hidden Persuaders*. New York, New York: David McKay Company Inc., 1961.

Reno, Dawn E. *The Confident Collector Advertising Identification and Price Guide*. New York, New York: Avon Books, 1993.

Robison, Joleen, and Kay Sellers. *Advertising Dolls: Identification and Value Guide*. Paducah, Kentucky: Collector Books, 1992.

Uston, Ken. *Mastering Pac-Man*. New York, New York: Signet Books-New American Library, 1982.

Welsh, David. *A Pictorial Guide to Plastic Candy Dispensers Featuring PEZ®*. Murphysboro, Illinois: Bubba Scrubba Publications, 1993.

INDEX

Books on Antiques and Collectibles

This is only a partial listing of the books on antiques that are available from Collector Books. All books are well illustrated and contain current values. Most of the following books are available from your local book seller, antique dealer, or public library. If you are unable to locate certain titles in your area, you may order by mail from COLLECTOR BOOKS, P.O. Box 3009, Paducah, KY 42002-3009. Customers with Visa or MasterCard may phone in orders from 8:00–4:00 CST, Monday–Friday, Toll Free 1-800-626-5420. Add $2.00 for postage for the first book ordered and $0.30 for each additional book. Include item number, title, and price when ordering. Allow 14 to 21 days for delivery.

BOOKS ON GLASS AND POTTERY

1810	American Art Glass, Shuman	$29.95
1312	Blue & White Stoneware, McNerney	$9.95
1959	Blue Willow, 2nd Ed., Gaston	$14.95
3719	Coll. Glassware from the 40's, 50's, 60's, 2nd Ed., Florence	$19.95
3816	Collectible Vernon Kilns, Nelson	$24.95
3311	Collecting Yellow Ware – Id. & Value Gd., McAllister	$16.95
1373	Collector's Ency. of American Dinnerware, Cunningham	$24.95
3815	Coll. Ency. of Blue Ridge Dinnerware, Newbound	$19.95
2272	Collector's Ency. of California Pottery, Chipman	$24.95
3811	Collector's Ency. of Colorado Pottery, Carlton	$24.95
3312	Collector's Ency. of Children's Dishes, Whitmyer	$19.95
2133	Collector's Ency. of Cookie Jars, Roerig	$24.95
3723	Coll. Ency. of Cookie Jars-Volume II, Roerig	$24.95
3724	Collector's Ency. of Depression Glass, 11th Ed., Florence	$19.95
2209	Collector's Ency. of Fiesta, 7th Ed., Huxford	$19.95
1439	Collector's Ency. of Flow Blue China, Gaston	$19.95
3812	Coll. Ency. of Flow Blue China, 2nd Ed., Gaston	$24.95
3813	Collector's Ency. of Hall China, 2nd Ed., Whitmyer	$24.95
2334	Collector's Ency. of Majolica Pottery, Katz-Marks	$19.95
1358	Collector's Ency. of McCoy Pottery, Huxford	$19.95
3313	Collector's Ency. of Niloak, Gifford	$19.95
3837	Collector's Ency. of Nippon Porcelain I, Van Patten	$24.95
2089	Collector's Ency. of Nippon Porcelain II, Van Patten	$24.95
1665	Collector's Ency. of Nippon Porcelain III, Van Patten	$24.95
1447	Collector's Ency. of Noritake, 1st Series, Van Patten	$19.95
1034	Collector's Ency. of Roseville Pottery, Huxford	$19.95
1035	Collector's Ency. of Roseville Pottery, 2nd Ed., Huxford	$19.95
3314	Collector's Ency. of Van Briggle Art Pottery, Sasicki	$24.95
3433	Collector's Guide To Harker Pottery - U.S.A., Colbert	$17.95
2339	Collector's Guide to Shawnee Pottery, Vanderbilt	$19.95
1425	Cookie Jars, Westfall	$9.95
3440	Cookie Jars, Book II, Westfall	$19.95
2275	Czechoslovakian Glass & Collectibles, Barta	$16.95
3882	Elegant Glassware of the Depression Era, 6th Ed., Florence	$19.95
3725	Fostoria - Pressed, Blown & Hand Molded Shapes, Kerr	$24.95
3883	Fostoria Stemware - The Crystal for America, Long	$24.95
3886	Kitchen Glassware of the Depression Years, 5th Ed., Florence	$19.95
3889	Pocket Guide to Depression Glass, 9th Ed., Florence	$9.95
3825	Puritan Pottery, Morris	$24.95
1670	Red Wing Collectibles, DePasquale	$9.95
1440	Red Wing Stoneware, DePasquale	$9.95
1958	So. Potteries Blue Ridge Dinnerware, 3rd Ed., Newbound	$14.95
3739	Standard Carnival Glass, 4th Ed., Edwards	$24.95
3327	Watt Pottery – Identification & Value Guide, Morris	$19.95
2224	World of Salt Shakers, 2nd Ed., Lechner	$24.95

BOOKS ON DOLLS & TOYS

2079	Barbie Fashion, Vol. 1, 1959-1967, Eames	$24.95
3310	Black Dolls – 1820 - 1991 – Id. & Value Guide, Perkins	$17.95
3810	Chatty Cathy Dolls, Lewis	$15.95
1529	Collector's Ency. of Barbie Dolls, DeWein	$19.95
2338	Collector's Ency. of Disneyana, Longest & Stern	$24.95
3727	Coll. Guide to Ideal Dolls, Izen	$18.95
3822	Madame Alexander Price Guide #19, Smith	$9.95
3732	Matchbox Toys, 1948 to 1993, Johnson	$18.95
3733	Modern Collector's Dolls, 6th series, Smith	$24.95
1540	Modern Toys, 1930 - 1980, Baker	$19.95
3824	Patricia Smith's Doll Values – Antique to Modern, 10th ed	$12.95
3826	Story of Barbie, Westenhouser, No Values	$19.95
2028	Toys, Antique & Collectible, Longest	$14.95
1808	Wonder of Barbie, Manos	$9.95
1430	World of Barbie Dolls, Manos	$9.95

OTHER COLLECTIBLES

1457	American Oak Furniture, McNerney	$9.95
3716	American Oak Furniture, Book II, McNerney	$12.95
2333	Antique & Collectible Marbles, 3rd Ed., Grist	$9.95
1748	Antique Purses, Holiner	$19.95
1426	Arrowheads & Projectile Points, Hothem	$7.95
1278	Art Nouveau & Art Deco Jewelry, Baker	$9.95
1714	Black Collectibles, Gibbs	$19.95
1128	Bottle Pricing Guide, 3rd Ed., Cleveland	$7.95
3717	Christmas Collectibles, 2nd Ed., Whitmyer	$24.95
1752	Christmas Ornaments, Johnston	$19.95
3718	Collectible Aluminum, Grist	$16.95
2132	Collector's Ency. of American Furniture, Vol. I, Swedberg	$24.95
2271	Collector's Ency. of American Furniture, Vol. II, Swedberg	$24.95
3720	Coll. Ency. of American Furniture, Vol III, Swedberg	$24.95
3722	Coll. Ency. of Compacts, Carryalls & Face Powder Boxes, Mueller	$24.95
2018	Collector's Ency. of Granite Ware, Greguire	$24.95
3430	Coll. Ency. of Granite Ware, Book 2, Greguire	$24.95
1441	Collector's Guide to Post Cards, Wood	$9.95
2276	Decoys, Kangas	$24.95
1629	Doorstops – Id. & Values, Bertoia	$9.95
1716	Fifty Years of Fashion Jewelry, Baker	$19.95
3817	Flea Market Trader, 9th Ed., Huxford	$12.95
3731	Florence's Standard Baseball Card Price Gd., 6th Ed.	$9.95
3819	General Store Collectibles, Wilson	$24.95
3436	Grist's Big Book of Marbles, Everett Grist	$19.95
2278	Grist's Machine Made & Contemporary Marbles	$9.95
1424	Hatpins & Hatpin Holders, Baker	$9.95
3884	Huxford's Collectible Advertising – Id. & Value Gd., 2nd Ed	$24.95
3820	Huxford's Old Book Value Guide, 6th Ed.	$19.95
3821	Huxford's Paperback Value Guide	$19.95
1181	100 Years of Collectible Jewelry, Baker	$9.95
2216	Kitchen Antiques – 1790 - 1940, McNerney	$14.95
3887	Modern Guns – Id. & Val. Gd., 10th Ed., Quertermous	$12.95
3734	Pocket Guide to Handguns, Quertermous	$9.95
3735	Pocket Guide to Rifles, Quertermous	$9.95
3736	Pocket Guide to Shotguns, Quertermous	$9.95
2026	Railroad Collectibles, 4th Ed., Baker	$14.95
1632	Salt & Pepper Shakers, Guarnaccia	$9.95
1888	Salt & Pepper Shakers II, Guarnaccia	$14.95
2220	Salt & Pepper Shakers III, Guarnaccia	$14.95
3443	Salt & Pepper Shakers IV, Guarnaccia	$18.95
3890	Schroeder's Antiques Price Guide, 13th Ed.	$12.95
2096	Silverplated Flatware, 4th Ed., Hagan	$14.95
2348	20th Century Fashionable Plastic Jewelry, Baker	$19.95
3828	Value Guide to Advertising Memorabilia, Summers	$18.95
3830	Vintage Vanity Bags & Purses, Gerson	$24.95

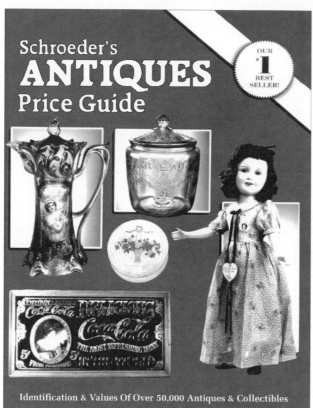